EZECHIEL

MAN OF SIGNS

By

DOM HUBERT VAN ZELLER

LONDON

SANDS & CO.

(PUBLISHERS) LIMITED

15 KING STREET, COVENT GARDEN, W.C.2

AND AT 76 CAMBRIDGE STREET, GLASGOW

1944

Nihil obstat: J. R. DAVEY,
             Censor Congr. Angliæ.

Imprimatur: H. BYRNE,
            Ab. Pres.

Nihil obstat: GEORGIUS CA. SMITH, S.M., Ph.D.,
            Censor deputatus.

Imprimatur: E. MORROGH BERNARD,
            Vic. Gen.

Westmonasterii, die 17 Februarii, 1944.

PRINTED IN GREAT BRITAIN BY
THE   STANHOPE PRESS LTD.
ROCHESTER   :   :   KENT

EZECHIEL

TO THE MEMORY OF
S. R. AND B. J.

CONTENTS

CHRONOLOGICAL TABLE

B.C.

c. 622   Birth of Ezechiel.

608   Death of Josias after defeat at Megiddo.

Joachaz reigns three months; is carried captive to Egypt.

Joachim, son of Josias, succeeds.

597   Joachim dethroned. Nabuchodonosor crowns his successor.

Joachim, son of Joachin, reigns for three months; is exiled.

Sedecias, son of Josias, succeeds.

592   Ezechiel is called by God.

588   Nabuchodonosor lays siege to Jerusalem.

587   Ezechiel's wife dies.

586   Nabuchodonosor destroys Jerusalem.

Sedecias is dethroned, blinded and exiled.

570   Last of Ezechiel's prophecies.

c. 569   Death of Ezechiel.

563   Release of Joachin from prison in Babylon.

INTRODUCTION

I ONCE heard someone—a most unlikely person—saying that he wished the Book of Ezechiel could be brought more to the notice of the present-day public. 'Because,' was the reason given, 'of that bit about the bones.' At that time I do not think I had read Ezechiel properly, and so knew nothing of the bones. One had heard the Prophecy read aloud, of course, in monastic choirs and refectories, but the general impression then received had been one of a bewildering mass of wheels, wings, clouds, cedar-trees, cherubims and complicated measurements. Having since studied the bit about the bones, I see why my friend wanted the Prophecy to be given a better press. This book is, accordingly, an attempt to revive interest in the prophet and his work.

It will be noticed that one or two side-lines which are considered by the scholars to be of paramount importance in any study of the Prophecy have, by me, been left out. For instance I have not drawn attention to the strangeness of the phrase 'son of man' (which occurs nearly a hundred times in Ezechiel and only once elsewhere in the Old Testament); nor has the prophet's theological thought been expressly gone into; textual questions have also been shelved. My excuse is that the pages which follow are intended to be primarily biographical. In the sense that Macaulay said of Boswell that he was the first of biographers I am prepared to write myself down as the last; but while allowing that I frequently wander from my subject I do still claim that this book is a life and not a scientific treatise. For those who want to study the Prophecy and its writer in greater detail there are excellent expositions on the market. The authors whose names appear in the Bibliography at the end will satisfy the keenest appetite for further knowledge, and to them I hereby express myself deeply indebted.

I submit what follows—slight though it is—to the absolute authority of the Holy See.

CHAPTER I

THE APPROACH

I

A BOOK, unless it happens to be a mystery novel, should give some sort of idea in the first chapter as to what it is going to be about. It is not the work of the chapter headings to tell the reader what to expect of the whole; nor should the last page be a temptation to the inquisitive student who hesitates at the first. In the briefest outline, then, the story of Ezechiel and his Prophecy is as follows:

Ezechiel (the name means 'God strengthens') was born in the seventh century B.C. We have no certain record of his birth, as we have no certain record of his death, but it is probable that the year 622 saw the beginning, and 569-8 the end, of Ezechiel's well-filled life.[1] This means that Ezechiel lived for about fifty-five years, thirty of which were spent in serving God as a prophet.

The name of Ezechiel's father was Buzi; about Buzi nothing whatever is known, but the family is believed to have been of the line of Zadoc. The Bene-Zadok ministered in the Temple at Jerusalem, and were therefore of the priestly succession. Certainly Ezechiel was a priest; he says so.[2] Certainly too he was, even after his exile from Jerusalem, comfortably off. He was an educated man and he was married. His Prophecy shows the fruit of either extensive reading or wide travel. And since his exile would have precluded the latter, we can assume that he devoted himself to the former. Certainly his know-

[1] The latest recorded date in the Prophecy is 570 ('the seven and twentieth year'—of the exile); the prophet is believed to have died quite soon after this.

[2] But even had he not said so we should have guessed it. The Prophecy shows the fullest knowledge of the Law, of ritual observances, of all kinds of Temple usage; see chapters xlii, xliii, xliv, xlvi.

ledge of both past history and contemporary affairs was considerable. The prophet's years of upbringing and preparation for the priesthood were spent at Jerusalem. The greater part of his life was lived in Chaldea, where, as an exile, he found a home—if it can be called a home— among the expatriated Jews who were allowed to settle and to make for themselves a colony of their own not far from Babylon. First on the banks of the river Chobar, and later at Tel-Abib, Ezechiel was granted his visions and revelations from the Lord. It was not until he was settled at Tel-Abib that he was launched upon his apostolate, and it is from that time onwards that the material of the Prophecy is mostly drawn. It was at Tel-Abib that Ezechiel wrote his book, and it was here too—or at Birs-Nimrod, which was not far away—that he finally met his death. So much for the man; the work he did may be summarised in the same way.

II

The Prophecy which bears his name was written down by Ezechiel after—perhaps long after—the events which it records. Some commentators would hold that Ezechiel, above all the literary prophet, produced his work in written form straight away, and that he never spoke a line of the discourses which it claims to report. There is no evidence to show for this; in fact, all the stock indications—style, character of the events narrated, arrangement of subject matter, graphic touches here and there, oratorical flourishes and whatnot—seem to point the other way. The Prophecy, as we shall see, was not well received either by the public to which he addressed himself immediately, or by the public at home in Jerusalem. We have to bear in mind when reading Ezechiel that the prophet was for ever looking over the shoulders

of his audience when speaking in Tel-Abib; he seems to
have felt more deeply the sufferings of those who had not
been turned out of their homes than the sufferings of
those who had. Perhaps he knew in his heart of hearts
that his fellow exiles, though shockingly unresponsive to
his appeals and inclined always to adapt themselves to
Babylonian manners, were of better stuff than were the
Jews at home; with the result that his major worries were
centred round the Temple court. 'By the waters of
Babylon we sat and wept . . . if I forget thee, O Jerusalem,
let my right hand be forgotten.'[1] But there was enough
to cause Ezechiel to sit and weep had he had no care for
Jerusalem; and if there was little chance of his forgetting
the Holy City, there was still less chance of his forgetting
Tel-Abib. The Jews of Tel-Abib saw to that.

Many reasons can be suggested as to why the Prophecy
was unpopular. It was unpopular chiefly because it was
impolite. People seem to think, looking back upon the
history of that time, that Ezechiel's thought was too
abstruse for the rude minds of the men of his age. This
is all nonsense. Ezechiel's thought is easy enough to
follow; it is the man's imagination which makes one
think he is soaring over people's heads. It is the tracery,
not the teaching, which gives the impression of obscurity;
and the tracery would not have seemed nearly so over-
done to the Eastern mind then as it does to the Western
mind now. Even today, when the literary taste of Palestine and Syria is considerably affected by the French
novel translated into Arabic, the Oriental mind takes
readily to symbolism and elaborate allegory. No, Ezechiel
was understood well enough—or he would not have been
so hotly resented. It is quite likely that the poetry was too
poetic and the prose too prosaic to be uproariously

[1] Psalm cxxxvi; 1, 5.

popular, but the Book as a whole was sufficiently clear to be rejected for its reactionary tendencies. In this strange Prophecy mysticism and mathematics went hand in hand; neither found acceptance among the Jews. Ezechiel's influence, like that of Jeremias, his contemporary across the desert, was destined to affect a chosen few. His vocation seems to have been to prepare a faithful minority which would, surviving the period of purification and handing down their tradition from father to son, inherit the blessings of the restoration and form the nucleus of the redeemed Kingdom. Such seems to have been Ezechiel's God-given purpose. That he must—with such a pro-gramme in front of him—have been a man of tremendous hope goes without saying; that he was a man also of colossal imagination and quite astonishing bravery will be shown, I hope, in the course of this book. How far he was successful in what he undertook can never, with entire satisfaction, be estimated: in this world we can at best get only a rough idea of the value to the Church of any one of her saints. Statistics show us something, but the true measure of a prophet's effect upon his people is bound—since we have only finite standards to go by— to escape us.

III

A word must be said on the prophet's mode of delivery: he acted his sermons. Again this would hardly have been considered peculiar in his own day, odd as it would have appeared to us. Where we, witnessing Ezechiel's un-ashamed demonstrations, would label the man a freak, the Jews, accustomed to that sort of thing from their prophets (but never getting so much of it as they got from Ezechiel), would take it all very much for granted as part of the preacher's stock-in-trade. I have ventured to call Ezechiel the 'man of signs' because this tendency to act is more marked in his case than it is in any of his predecessors: signs in the sense of gestures, not in the sense of wonders. These signs of his attracted ridicule, attracted hostility, attracted speculation, attracted interest, attracted protests of indifference, attracted crowds, attracted stones, but we are never told that they attracted surprise. And in the end he seems to have given them up. Presumably this was because in the end his signs were, together with the rest of his sermons, ignored. After his death—quite soon after his death—Ezechiel's name was honoured; men saw that they had frowned upon and smiled at (but for all practical purposes ignored) a saint. That is what happens to prophets and saints: they are despised in their lifetimes and loaded with honours afterwards. Another common thing which we find in the lives of saints and prophets is the violence of their deaths. The grace of martyrdom is said, though there is no certain evidence to prove it, to have been granted to the prophet Ezechiel. Whether or not a martyr, he is recognised by the Church as a saint. [1] So it is as gratifying to know that he was worthy of his palm as it is maddening to find no historical grounds for giving it to him. Since it is in the dress of a prophet, then, that Ezechiel is ordinarily put before us, it will be by his Prophecy (and not by his possible martyrdom or certain sanctity) that we shall take our stand.

Of the books which are given us from the pens of the major prophets, this one (Ezechiel's) should be the easiest to follow page by page. In Isaias and Jeremias the chronology is bewildering. Daniel groups his prophecies on a curious system of his own. Ezechiel is the only one who arranges his sermons in the order of their delivery,

[1] The Roman Martyrology celebrates the feast of the prophet Ezechiel on the tenth of April.

and he seems to be just as careful where it is a question of actual events. We have already touched upon the problem as to how much of the text represents the spoken word; we need add only that whereas commentators are agreed that the Prophecy was issued finally in written form, they are not agreed as to whether the individual prophecies came out bit by bit or whether they were saved up by Ezechiel and published at the end of his life. Once granted that the prophet's message was as much to the Jews at home as to the exiles at Tel-Abib, it seems more reasonable to allow that Ezechiel sent off his sermons to Jerusalem fairly soon after he had preached them. This would surely have been the case at the earlier stages; what he did later on we do not know, but (as will be seen in a later chapter) there is nothing to prevent his sitting down after his final vision and re-editing *all* his former work. There is much autobiographical material which would fittingly find a place in some such general revision that would perhaps have been out of tune in short separate issues. At all events, it will be our business here to trace the prophet's life through the sequence of his prophecies. By taking the Prophecy bit by bit, and noting the effect which its inspiration had upon himself as well as upon his public, we shall be able to form some sort of picture of the whole; it is only when we have made as sure as we can about the history that we can indulge ourselves in making shots about the possibilities. The way in which the final edition of the Prophecy was received by the Chosen People is, when all is said, still in the region of the 'possibilities.'

Before leaving this general and rather scrappy introduction it would be as well to note that the Book as we have it divides itself into two sections of almost identical length: the first part dealing with the fall of the Kingdom, the second with its revival. The last half can be further split up into more or less equal sections: the first outlining the preparation necessary for the nation's re-birth, the second telling what it will be like when it is re-born. For all his imagination and mystic temper Ezechiel is a most methodical person; he is as anxious as any sub-editor that the work should be tidy when it leaves the printers. Ezechiel is a man of letters as well as a man of God.

There will be no attempt in the pages which follow to give a running commentary on the text; it is far more my aim to give a walking character-sketch of the man. It would only be tedious and pedantic to develop this book along the lines of a glorified foot-note. More than anything else it is the story of Ezechiel which we are following. But let it be said with the utmost emphasis that the story here presented will be, as far as it is possible to give it, the true one.

IV

Jerusalem fell into the hands of Nabuchodonosor king of Babylon in the year 597 B.C. This was not the occasion of Jerusalem's destruction; another taking of the Holy City was to intervene before it should finally be sacked by Babylonian armies. All three sieges were conducted by Nabuchodonosor. We shall have cause to mention the two later campaigns on another page; it is the first which concerns us at the moment. For a considerable time before Jerusalem's first fall Babylon and Egypt had been menacing, the former from the east, the latter from the south, the borders of Judean territory. In 608 B.C. Pharaoh-Nechao defeated Juda's army at Megiddo and slew Josias the last of Jerusalem's worthy kings. The Egyptian was in his turn beaten at Carchemesh by Nabuchodonosor three years later, and thereafter appears no more on our horizon. But in the interval of

Josias's death and Nechao's defeat, Joachaz, son of Josias, reigned for three months over Jerusalem and then was sent off as an exile to Egypt. After him came Joachim, his brother, upon the throne, and it was during this man's reign that Egypt was overthrown by Babylon. The result was that Egypt's possessions, first among which was the kingdom of Juda, fell into the hands of Nabuchodonosor; Joachim, from being Pharaoh-Nechao's vassal, became Nabuchodonosor's vassal. All might have been well for Jerusalem had not Joachim, after fourteen years of quasi kingship (eleven years under Egypt, three under Babylon) rebelled against Nabuchodonosor. This brings us abreast of the date mentioned in the first line of this section: Nabuchodonosor took Jerusalem in 597 and dethroned the rebel king. As successor to Joachim the Babylonian monarch nominated and crowned Joachin, aged eighteen, as king of Juda. This was a handsome show of political goodwill because there was little enough reason to expect loyalty from the royal blood of Juda: Joachin was the son of one rebel and the nephew of another. The experiment was a failure; the reign lasted a bare three months. Jeremias (who, it must be admitted, had a rooted objection to the whole family—with the exception, of course, of the devout Josias) calls Joachin 'an earthen and a broken vessel,' and says that none of his seed shall inherit. [1] The surrender of Joachin is piteous: he went

[1] Jeremias had advised Joachim to side with Babylon but had not been listened to. He had then urged the same king to read his (Jeremias's) prophecies; again he had been turned down. In 597 he preached openly against giving to Joachim the funeral rites due to a dead king. Of the son he says 'write this man barren', and his injunction was justified: Joachin, though he lived to be released from his captivity, could give no sons to Juda's throne. Nor did he, in spite of the hopes held out by the false prophets whom Ezechiel and Jeremias attacked with equal force, return again to his native Juda. This king comes into the story again—when we come to deal at the end with the legend attaching to Ezechiel's death and burial.

out to meet Nabuchodonosor with a whole party of shame-faced hangers-on, 'he and his mother and his servants, and his nobles, and his eunuchs . . . and the king of Babylon received him.' The same account (from the Book of Kings [1]) goes on to say that Joachin gave up the trea-sures of the Temple and the palace, and that Nabu-chodonosor 'carried away all the princes and the valiant men of the army . . . and he carried away Joachin into Babylon, and the king's mother, and the king's wives and his eunuchs; and the judges of the land he carried away into captivity from Jerusalem into Babylon.' This phase has been dealt with here because it was in the deportation just mentioned that Ezechiel was carried away captive. Jeremias remained on in Jerusalem. To complete our survey of Judean affairs at this period it is necessary only to say that in Joachin's stead, Sedecias (another son of Josias) was placed by Nabuchodonosor upon the throne of Juda. This king reigned (very badly) for eleven years; in the ninth year of Sedecias's reign Nabu-chodonosor laid the second siege of Jerusalem, and in the eleventh year he laid a third. Even Nabuchodonosor's patience was exhausted; in 586 Jerusalem was utterly destroyed, Sedecias was dethroned and blinded, and no more kings were suffered to assume the dishonoured purple. The kingdom was at an end.

V

We shall now have to go back, for the space of a single chapter, and consider what were the feelings of Ezechiel during all this period of Juda's changing fortune. When we have dealt with what we think he felt before his deportation we shall be in a better position to understand what we know he felt after it.

[1] 4 Kings xxiv, 12-16.

CHAPTER II

THE SETTING

I

IF EZECHIEL was born when we think he was, and if he was allowed as a boy to interest himself in the political changes which were taking place all round him, then it is obvious from what has been said that the prophet's early years were exciting years. As a child he would have come under the influence of Josias's educational reforms. As a growing youth he would have had to make careful preparation for the priesthood. Study—and particularly religious study—would have been the normal atmosphere in which he moved. He would have heard much about the leading prophet of his day—Jeremias. He may even have studied under the senior prophet in the Temple schools, where Jeremias seems for a time to have held the post of lecturer. Living within the same city walls as Jeremias, Ezechiel would have kindled from the other's fiery zeal that flame which was to burn its way through the dried up vegetation of his future exile. The two men had much in common: both were enthusiasts, both were educated in the Law, both were poets of a distinctly high order, both were—ultimately—exiles and probably martyrs. Jeremias left Jerusalem for Egypt, Ezechiel left Jerusalem for Babylon. Both of them left Jerusalem for good. One wonders how far each was able to follow the other's career. There is no reason why they should not have corresponded; there was plenty to correspond about. [1]

[1] 'How constant the intercourse was between Jerusalem and the Jewish colonies in Babylonia, we may see, not only from Ezechiel but from Jeremiah. In Jeremiah xxix we have the substance of a letter sent by Jeremiah through two royal officials to the exiles exhorting them to resign themselves to the will of God and obey their foreign lords in spite of the misleading advice of the lower prophets. On the receipt of this, one of the latter wrote letters to the Jews at home.' Cheyne, *Jeremiah*, p. 169.

If there are grounds for believing that Ezechiel and Jeremias were friends, there are surer grounds for postulating a friendship between Ezechiel and Daniel. They were more of the same age, they had studied under the same doctors, they were exiled to the same country. Daniel does not mention Ezechiel but Ezechiel mentions Daniel—twice. Daniel was exiled by Nabuchodonosor during Joachim's reign, Ezechiel followed some years later. Daniel, from the time of his arrival in the Chaldean capital, spent many years in the service of one or other of Babylon's kings and died in the reign of Cyrus the Persian. This means that he outlived Ezechiel, and witnessed the deliverance of the Jews from their captivity. He was still alive in 536, the date of Babylon's fall. The two men had the same difficulties to face, but under a different form: difficulties arising from a prolonged and a not very exacting exile. We find that after the first ache of loneliness had passed, the Jews settled down only too well in their new surroundings, and showed no great desire to go back. The problem which Ezechiel had to face was that of how to convince his people that their exile would be a long one; the problem which Daniel had to face was that of how to convince his people that their exile was not going to last for ever. Where Daniel had to stimulate homesickness, Ezechiel had to stifle it.

II

Ezechiel was evidently a man who could be influenced on the surface by surrounding circumstances. Though possessed of a certain individuality, Ezechiel will be seen to reflect the mood of the time and place in which he finds himself. Thus his poetry—not, of course, his theology—is coloured by the imagery of Babylon, while his thought

is reminiscent of the prophets who have gone before.[1]
His Prophecy is a blending of divers responses to divers
stimuli. Not all light, not all shadow. In the first half of
the Book he reflects the gloom, in the second the hope,
of the Chosen People. So if as a grown man he was
sensitive to outward things, what must he not have felt
as a child with regard to the events which we have out-
lined above? He would have wept when everyone else
wept at the obsequies of Josias;[2] he would have endured
the miseries which the devout among Juda's people
endured under the successive rules of the inept kings
Joachaz and Joachim; he would have felt keenly the
departure of Daniel; and finally he would have had to
say goodbye to Jerusalem himself. Mostly in shadow,
then, were the first twenty-five years of Ezechiel's life;
the one ray of light seems to have been his marriage, and
then in his early thirties his wife died. No wonder that
even his later work was to savour somewhat of melancholy:
the man was old before his time. Not so old that he could
no longer be enthusiastic about the things which mattered, but old enough to have passed through his novitiate
of suffering.

III

If we were to transport ourselves in spirit to Chaldea
in the January or February of the year 696 B.C. we should
find that Ezechiel and his fellow exiles have just about
arrived at the place of their first detention. For the time
being it has been arranged that the Hebrews should be

---

[1] Ezechiel owes most to Jeremias, but there are traces of Isaias, Osee,
Amos and Micheas.

[2] Jerusalem mourned generously for Josias. Popular dirges were sung
in the streets, and certain lamentations (composed almost certainly by
Jeremias) were introduced into the Temple liturgy and kept up for some
weeks.

billeted by the river Chobar.[1] Permanent quarters were
being got ready farther south, where a Jewish colony was
to be formed. In the meantime Jewish labour came in
very useful for the gigantic building and irrigation
enterprises which were being undertaken in and about
Babylon. Perhaps Nabuchodonosor kept the Jews at
Chobar so as to employ them in widening the canal
and bringing the mud to the capital; the canals of Chaldea
were as much used as the roads, and the mud would have
been wanted for the walls and gardens which were being
altered at this time. How long the exiles had to remain
at Chobar we do not know, but it was probably about
two years before they were allowed to go on and build
houses of their own at Tel-Abib.

It is not hard to imagine the kinds of letters which
would have followed the Jews across the desert. The
hostesses in Jerusalem would have written to their exiled
friends saying how hopeless the business of entertaining
had become under the Chaldean occupation . . . the
season quite ruined . . . nothing but Babylonians everywhere, with their bad manners and ugly beards . . . and
Jeremias telling everyone that things would get worse.
We can imagine also that from the more serious-minded
in Jerusalem letters would have reached Chobar telling
the dispersed how unsatisfactory Sedecias was proving
himself as king . . . how right Jeremias had been after all
. . . how slender seemed the chances of ever throwing off
the yoke of Babylon.

Not difficult either to imagine the kind of reply which

[1] The text of Ezechiel mentions 'the river Chobar,' but in point of strict
fact it seems to have been a man-made canal. It led off the Euphrates
and irrigated the plains east of the capital. The Chobar has been identified
with the present Shatt-en-Nil. The canal today measures about 120 feet
across; it is strange to think of the prophet being employed on the work of
repairing its banks or enlarging its tributaries.

would have left by messenger from Chobar or Tel-Abib. It wasn't so much (an exile correspondent might have answered) that Chaldea was insupportable, it was simply that one longed to be at home instead of in a foreign suburb. True, one could amuse oneself in Babylon from time to time, but one felt so *out of it* when one did. Then there was the language problem. If only Chaldean could be picked up quickly there wouldn't be these difficulties about the children's lessons, about the housekeeping, about doing a little trade in a quiet way. Soon one would have to start picking up the social thread again, one supposed, but really one hardly felt up to it just at present. How *very* different everything was here from what it used to be in the old days at home. Certainly the Chaldeans were pretty barbarous. Was it known in Jerusalem, for instance, that Babylonian women actually worked in the market places? In fact they seemed to do everything just like the men, and wore the *oddest* clothes. [1] An interesting sidelight on the state of affairs here was the respect with which Daniel was regarded. (Only there was strong opposition, of course, from some quarters—noticeably from among the 'elders.') Unfortunately the Chaldeans seemed to expect an equally high standard from the rest of us. That was the worst of these holy people—they made things so impossible for everyone else. The opinion among the Hebrews at present was (one was glad to say) that the less fuss about religion the better. Only it would be as well not to mention this fact to Jeremias: another tirade would be most inopportune. He and Ezechiel made things so much more complicated than they needed to be.

[1] The women of Babylon did not wear the veil. The only aspect of Babylonian life from which women were excluded was the banquet. It appears that in allowing his nobles to bring their womenfolk to his feast, Baltassar was introducing something new.

Perhaps Ezechiel would get less zealous as he grew older; after all, he was only in his early twenties and not yet a qualified priest.[2] It was such a pity that his dear little wife agreed with every word the man said. But then she was another one of these holy people, and so delicate too.

In some such form as this letters would have been exchanged between the separated communities during the early years of the Captivity. It did not take long for Nabuchodonosor's handling of the Jewish situation to have effect. Geographically the people of Israel were cut off from their centre; constitutionally they were rendered impotent. No national or religious revival could be initiated by a people who were forbidden to elect their own governors, to build their own tabernacles, to keep their own feasts, to frame their own laws. Exiled Israel sought consolation from Babylon; the pure water of Jordan flowed easily into the polluted torrent of the Euphrates. Over the desert came the strident voice of Jeremias in protest. A deaf ear was turned. The voice of Ezechiel—a more halting voice, as we shall see— echoed that of Jeremias. Again a deaf ear was turned. To the Jews of Tel-Abib the word of God was an echo of an echo, and excuses were found to evade even that.

[2] According to the law a man did not become a priest until he was thirty years of age. So if Ezechiel was exiled at twenty-five he would at this time still have been ministering as an assistant at whatever rites were possible of practice in Chaldea. In point of fact it seems that there was little enough that a priest might do outside Palestine. 'Exile necessarily entailed a suspension of sacrifice. Popular Jahwism, as practised by most of the Jews in Egypt, managed to avoid this result by bringing earth from Palestine and building an altar upon it.' Lods, *The Prophets and The Rise of Judaism*, p. 218. Unless the exiles in Chaldea resorted to some such expedient, religious worship must have come almost to a standstill.

CHAPTER III

THE CALL

I

'Now it came to pass in the thirtieth year, in the fourth month, on the fifth day of the month, when I was in the midst of the captives by the river Chobar, the heavens were opened and I saw the visions of God. On the fifth day of the month, the same was the fifth year of the captivity of king Joachin, the word of the Lord came to Ezechiel the son of Buzi in the land of the Chaldeans by the river Chobar; and the hand of the Lord was there upon him. And I saw, and behold a whirlwind came out of the north, and a great cloud and a fire enfolding it, and brightness was about it; and out of the midst thereof—that is out of the midst of the fire—as it were the resemblance of amber; and in the midst thereof the likeness of four living creatures. . . .'

Then follows a longish account of the prophet's vision. In the divided heavens he was given to see many strange things: a chariot racing through space, 'wheels lifted up' and 'dreadful of appearance,' 'living creatures' which ran and flashed like lightning, a luminous cloud, a firmament terrible to behold, a tumult of many waters, and—unexpectedly after all this violent action—a rainbow. Within this last—'as the appearance of a rainbow when it is in a cloud on a rainy day'—Ezechiel beheld 'the Glory of the Lord.' 'And I saw,' says the prophet, 'and I fell upon my face, and I heard the voice of one that spoke.'

But before we consider what it was that Ezechiel heard, it is worth while noticing how very exact, considering he is a visionary, the prophet is; he gives us the year and the

month and the day, and tells us where he was at the time.
These references to Ezechiel's accuracy will be met with
fairly often in this book—the idea being that we shall
have something to go upon when the possibility of there
being two Ezechiels is considered. Critics, it must be
stated at the outset, are always in favour of multiplying
their sacred writers wherever possible. They split up
Isaias, Daniel, Habacuc and Zacharias, so it is natural
for them to want—where so much ground exists for doing
it—to split up Ezechiel also. Thus we have the matter-
of-fact Ezechiel (the recorder who wrote rather heavy
prose) and the imaginative enthusiast Ezechiel (who
wrote the highest mystical poetry). The opening passage
of the Prophecy is significant in this respect, and that is
why the dual authorship question is brought up here.
Consider the material which is provided in those first few
sentences which we have quoted. He was, he tells us,
grown up. (There is to be no question afterwards of
childish daydreams or anything of that sort; he was
thirty years old when the vision appeared to him.) He
was, he implies, though does not state it in as many words,
a priest. Part of the Jewish colony was still, it seems, at
Chobar. Joachin had been nearly five years a prisoner.
And finally, as we have pointed out, he gives the exact
date. There is no doubt about it, documentation is one
of Ezechiel's strong points. He may be eccentric as an
orator, but he is businesslike as a biographer.

Myself, I consider the dual authorship theory to be the
completest rubbish—as also I consider that theory which
makes this and other of Ezechiel's visions the result of a
mental process known as a 'trance-reflex.'[1] One would

[1] The suggestion is that Ezechiel, a highly imaginative subject in any
case, would, when he gave himself to prayer, have *fancied* a number of
objects which would normally have been connected in his mind with the
idea of God. Thus from a study of Babylon's temples, for instance, the

have thought that no fair-minded reader of the first
and second chapters of Ezechiel could doubt the matter
for a moment. If this is not a supernatural visitation,
what is? You might as well put down St. Peter's vision of
'unclean' food to his feeling hungry, or St. John's vision
of stars and candlesticks to his feeling sleepy. Ezechiel's
overwhelming experience at Chobar is either a God-given
ecstasy or a deliberately man-made fantasy; it is certainly
not a fortuitous afternoon reverie.

As to what was said to the prophet 'out of the brightness
round about,' these were the instructions he received.
(The passage must be quoted in full because of its bearing
both upon Ezechiel's prophetical career and upon Juda's
attitude of heart.)

> 'Son of man, [said the One that spoke] I send
> thee to the children of Israel, to a rebellious people
> that hath revolted from Me; they and their fathers
> have transgressed My covenant even unto this day.
> And they to whom I send thee are children of a
> hard face and an obstinate heart. And thou shalt
> say to them: Thus saith the Lord God: If so be they
> at last will hear, and if so be they will forbear, for
> they are a provoking house, and they shall know
> that there hath been a prophet in the midst of them.
> And thou, O son of man, fear not, neither be thou
> afraid of their words; for thou art among unbelievers
> and destroyers, and thou dwellest with scorpions.
> Fear not their words neither be thou dismayed at

imagery of his vision would take what to him would be almost tangible
shape. From this it is no great step further to suggest (as the 'trance-
reflex' people further suggest) that the images which obsessed his mind
translated themselves automatically into the appropriate gestures or signs
to which the prophet was so much addicted. In other words the whole
thing (according to this school of psychologists) was a piece of self-hypnotism; perfectly sincere, perhaps, but self-hypnotism nevertheless.

their looks, for they are a provoking house. And thou shalt speak My words to them, if perhaps they will hear and forbear, for they provoke Me to anger. But thou, O son of man, hear all that I say to thee, and do not thou provoke Me as that house provoketh Me. Open thy mouth and eat what I give thee.'

We see at once that to preach to God's people is not going to be a very gratifying experience. The prophet seems to need propping up to meet each sentence in the statement of his commission. Fear not, they *are* a hard lot; don't be dismayed, they *do* look like scorpions; listen to what I say, don't *you* provoke Me to anger. . . . No, it was not an easy task that lay in front of the would-be reformer of exiled Israel. The people to whom Ezechiel was to address himself were most unwilling to receive, unless it came wrapped up in cotton wool, a message from the Lord. They expected to be told—as the false prophets in point of fact did tell them—that they would soon be going home. Ezechiel's business would be to explain that, far from going home just yet, they would have to endure the mortification of listening from afar to the tale of Jerusalem's burning. The Temple would be destroyed, the king would be dethroned, the nationality of Israel would come to an end. No wonder Ezechiel needed to be fortified by God. No wonder he viewed his task with a reluctance bordering almost on despair. 'But 'fear not, it is *I* that send thee' is the consolation which he may rest upon.

That a favoured soul should instinctively draw back when presented with a work to do for God is nothing outstanding in the history of spirituality. Scripture itself furnishes a number of examples. Moses, Jonas, Balaam, Habacuc were none too eager, while Jeremias's 'Ah, ah,

.h, Lord God, behold I cannot speak' is as famous as it is
cypical.[1] Up and down Ezechiel's Book we find evidence
to show that the prophet spoke only because he had to
and not because he wanted to. One wonders whether
this common experience among God's servants was at
the back of Chesterton's mind when, in his novel *The Man
Who Was Thursday*, he describes an interview between
the leader of a secret society and a candidate proposed
for membership. The dialogue runs as follows:

' "Are you the new recruit?" said the invisible chief,
who seemed to have heard all about it. "All right. You
are engaged."

Syme, quite swept off his feet, made a feeble fight
against this irrevocable phrase.

"I really have no experience," he began.

"No one has any experience," said the other, "of the
Battle of Armageddon."

"But I am really unfit——"

"You are willing, that is enough," said the unknown.

"Well, really," said Syme, "I don't know any profession of which mere willingness is the final test."

"I do," said the other, "martyrs. I am condemning
you to death. Good-day." '[2]

In the last analysis it seems that willingness *is* the only

[1] 'No Prophet took up his mission of his own will; it was imposed on
him as a necessity against which he fought in vain: "For prophecy came
not by the will of man at any time: but the holy men of God spoke, inspired
by the Holy Ghost . . ." There remains no other conclusion but that the
mission of the Prophets is a supernatural vocation, an immediate action of
God on their minds—often contrary to their natural inclinations—impelling
them to carry out His commands.' Dom Dominic Allen, *The Old Testament,
Cambridge Summer School Papers*, 1938.

[2] *Op. cit.* p. 82-3. To suggest that Chesterton had the prophets in mind
when he wrote these lines is not as fantastic as might at first appear. The
novel's concluding chapter shows very clearly that a Biblical parallel is
intended; the spirituality, in fact, which is to be found between pages
321-329 is as lofty as any mystic could wish to read.

test for the harder vocations; experience is not one of the requirements, and fitness is simply qualified by the subject's good will. Ezechiel may have trembled and recoiled, but the point was *he accepted*.

The detail of his being given a book to eat is not without its significance. Apart from the fact that it reminds us, of course, of the similar incident in the mystical experience of St. John (as described in the tenth chapter of the Apocalypse), it also marks out Ezechiel from his fellow prophets in a way which quite easily might be missed by a casual reading of his Prophecy. Let us look at the words which follow the passage already quoted.

> 'And I looked,' continues Ezechiel, 'and behold a hand was sent to me, wherein was a book rolled up. And He spread it before me, and it was written within and without, and there were written in it lamentations and canticles and woe. And He said to me: Son of man, eat all that thou shalt find: eat this book and go, speak to the children of Israel.'

The implication of this seems to be that with Ezechiel a new phase has begun in Hebrew prophecy: his is to be a literary conception of God's message. Hitherto the 'word of the Lord' had been preached freely under the influence of God's spirit; in Ezechiel's case there would be a *written* revelation. Inspiration, to Ezechiel, was to be delivered in book form. 'Jeremiah,' writes Loring W. Batten in his excellent work *The Hebrew Prophet*, 'had been sent about the country to preach the newly discovered book of Deuteronomy, but Ezechiel is commanded to eat a book containing the message he is to preach.'[1] It is almost as if the prophet had so far wilted under the shock of his commission that the Lord thought it well to nourish

[1] p. 99.

him supernaturally. And the substance of the nourishment was lamentation and woe![1]

Notice how the Voice insisted that it was the 'children of Israel' to whom Ezechiel was to 'go and speak'; not, that is, to anyone else. Other nations would misread God's message; Israel will read it aright—but will fail to respond. To *all* Israel, moreover, is the word addressed. Ezechiel must be listened to at home as well as locally in exile. To those of the captivity the prophet will find himself acting as a 'watchman,' a pastor, a chaplain, a spiritual director and a consoler, but the doctrine which is quite particularly *his* is a doctrine which must be learned by all Jehovah's sons. The principle that the soul has an individual responsibility before God is not for Chobar or Tel-Abib alone.

II

As in the case of the apostle John, so in the case of the apostle Ezechiel—the book which was eaten was as sweet as honey in the mouth. Thus refreshed, the prophet was again told that though his public would be of his own flesh and blood he was not to expect a better reception than might be extended by the heathen and the unbeliever; in fact, the opposite—'if thou wert sent to *them* they would hearken to thee.' But Israel had a 'hard forehead and an obstinate heart.' Again, Ezechiel was told not to be afraid, but simply to go ahead; the words which he would speak would be the words of God.

Following which, and presuming upon the prophet's consent, the Spirit of the Lord lifted the limp and fainting

[1] It is hardly necessary to mention the fact that the passage need not be pressed to mean the imposition of a document to be read out or even re-edited by Ezechiel when once his mission should be launched. It merely means that Ezechiel's particular contribution as a prophet was to be a literary one.

Ezechiel, and removed him from the scene of his initiation to the place of the proposed ministry. 'In bitterness,' Ezechiel tells us, he made this journey, but 'the hand of the Lord was with me, strengthening me.' Sweet was the word of the Lord when first perceived, but afterwards (as also in the case of John) the effect was bitter. So bitter did the prophet feel about the whole thing that when he arrived at Tel-Abib and actually saw his future congregation, his heart—also his voice and knees—failed him, and he sank down under the weight of the divine oppression. In our text the verse which describes this weakness is slightly corrupt; it should read 'I came to them of the captivity, to Tel-Abib where they dwelt, and I sat there dumb and motionless among them.'[1] Do we wonder at this lethargy? For five years he had looked with unseeing eyes upon his flock-to-be. And he had not thought much of them. He was now granted to look at them with spiritual insight and with a full knowledge of his destined relationship towards them. And he thought still less.

'At the end of seven days,' the text goes on, 'the word of the Lord came to me saying: Son of man, I have made thee a watchman to the house of Israel.' And the Lord proceeded to warn his servant that if, through the watchman's negligence, the divine message should fail to reach the ears of those for whom it was intended, the harm done to souls would be imputed to the prophet at the day of judgement. One feels for Ezechiel; what with physical exhaustion and mental stress, things were getting worse and worse. He seems to have made a seven days' retreat

[1] In the Vulgate there is no mention of Tel-Abib; it puts instead 'to the heap of new corn.' But the Hebrew for new corn in heaps *is* 'tel-abib.' So it looks as if the majority of the colonists went with Ezechiel from Chobar, the original settlement, to Tel-Abib. This is worth mentioning because some commentators identify the two places.

before this second phase of his experience. Just as Job settled down to listen for seven days to the mournings of his comforters, so Ezechiel settled down for the same time to consider the melancholy message of the Lord. Ezechiel's prophetical function, then, was now defined; he was, as a 'watchman,' to look out for the approaching doom, and, when he saw it coming, to warn the community of its imminence. The doom was of course the break-up of Israel.

Here the sequence of events becomes a little hard to follow; the next stage is described by the prophet like this:

> 'And the hand of the Lord was upon me, and He said to me: Rise and go forth unto the plain and there I will speak to thee. And I rose up and went forth into the plain, and behold the Glory of the Lord stood there, like the Glory which I saw by the river Chobar,[1] and I fell upon my face. And the Spirit entered into me and set me upon my feet, and He spoke to me and said to me: Go in and shut thyself up in the midst of thy house. And thou, son of man, behold they shall put bands upon thee and they shall bind thee with them, and thou shalt not go forth from the midst of them. And I will make thy tongue stick fast to the roof of thy mouth and thou shalt be dumb . . . but when I shall speak to thee I will open thy mouth, and thou shalt say to them: Thus saith the Lord God: He that heareth, let him hear. . . .'

Commentators find different explanations to the above

---

[1] Which again shows that the Jews, Ezechiel among them, no longer inhabited the first place of their exile; if the reference does not exactly prove this, it at least differentiates between the two localities, Chobar and Tel-Abib.

passage. Some have taken it to mean that the Lord simply repeated the vision and then told Ezechiel to continue his retreat—this time within the enclosure of his own home. Others (with, to my mind, less justification) consider that the prophet began his work, proved himself a failure, and was instructed to abandon the active ministry for the time being.[1] Since the point is not vital, and since the scholars are found to disagree, I humbly submit that the text allows of the following interpretation: God revealed His Glory to Ezechiel in the open plain; then, so that Ezechiel might have greater privacy and freedom from distraction in order to consider what he had seen and was now about to hear, He told him to go indoors; once settled within his own walls, Ezechiel was forewarned of the kind of thing which he was to expect in connexion with his apostolate—which things would set the seal of authenticity to all that had gone before. The prophet would, for example, be ill used by his flock; he would find himself, moreover, unable to speak properly. This last circumstance would not be due to natural infirmity, but to the direct supernatural operation of God. A sign which might be taken to show that the dumbness was not something purely physical was the fact that 'when I, God, shall speak to thee, thou shalt say: Thus saith the Lord God, etc.'

But whether this is the best rendering of the prophet's meaning or not, the drift of the passage is clear. The revelation amounts to a much emphasised injunction *not to give up in the face of apparent failure.* 'You will have to drop all preaching for a time,' says the Lord in effect, 'because when the people are not putting you under restraint I shall be putting you under My own ban of

---

[1] See Davidson and Streane, *Cambridge Bible*, pp. 28, 29.

C—e

silence. You will feel this impotence, this seeming failure
to realise what you consider to be an essential feature of
your vocation. You will want to express yourself, and
you will be unable to. You will burn with an increasing
zeal for souls, and you will find yourself proportionately
blocked in their service. You will think that your new-
found talents are being wasted. You will feel broken,
discouraged, finished. But whatever the extent of your
apparent failure, you are not to give up. I, the Lord,
have spoken: *Thou shalt not go forth from the midst of these
people.* Your real work for Me will only really *begin* when
all these things shall come upon you. So when these
things come upon you, don't imagine that your work for
Me is finished merely because your plans for Me have
failed. Failure, O son of man, is often the hall-mark of
true success, while success is often the cloak of inward
failure.' This would have been clear enough to Ezechiel
had he been able, when he 'shut himself up in the midst
of his house,' to take a copy of the New Testament with
him. Had he been able, further, to take a volume of
Mr. Belloc's collected poems with him into his retreat,
he would surely have derived great consolation from the
verse which runs:

> *Prince, may I venture (since it's only you)*
> *To speak discreetly of the Crucified?*
> *He was extremely unsuccessful too:*
> *The Devil didn't like Him, and He died.*

CHAPTER IV

EZECHIEL'S DUMBNESS

THE account of the inaugural vision (or rather, group of visions) closes with Ezechiel's third chapter. The next part of the Prophecy goes on to describe the practical unfolding of the prophet's spiritual commission. But before we consider how Ezechiel went about his labours we can suitably devote a few pages to the discussion of this 'dumbness' on which stress was laid by the Lord in the calling of Ezechiel to the work of prophecy. Twice already we have been told that he was rendered speechless, and we shall meet it twice again.[1] It is true that at the beginning, when the 'visions of God' first appeared to him, Ezechiel was so thunderstruck, *naturally speaking*, that he would have described himself afterwards as having been 'unable to say a word' at the time. The combined influence of surprise, awe, fear, dread of the consequences, and so on, would have been quite enough to account for the state if that was all we were told about it. But the tongue-tied condition which is spoken of by the Lord to Ezechiel—apart from that which is spoken of by Ezechiel to his readers—is quite another matter.

Was this dumbness simply a sort of stutter (as it seems to have been in the case of Moses) intended to rob him of any pretensions towards being a successful preacher? Was it the kind of thing we read about in the Book of Job, for instance, and in Lamentations and Psalms?[2] Did it apply to *all* human intercourse, or did the dumbness come on only when there was question of reproving Israel for its sins? Was it perhaps a way of keeping the prophet from saying too much?

[1] xxiv, 27; xxxiii, 22.
[2] Job xxix, 10; Lamentations iv, 4; Psalms xxi, 16.

What follows by way of answer to these questions is necessarily conjectural, but in the process of arriving at our main conclusion we can—even if the conclusion itself be not accepted very generally—dispose of much confused thought upon the subject of Ezechiel's dumbness. In the first place we can surely take it for granted that the prophet was able to get on all right in ordinary intercourse on secular matters. There is no reason to think that he was unable, for instance, to order his household provisions by word of mouth. We must remember that the whole thing was from God, and that it affected the things of God. The particular significance of the affliction would have been entirely missed if the impediment had equally affected the things of man. Again, that it was not merely a case of a very pronounced stutter is clear from the twofold fact that it induced silence, and that it did so in a way which was recognisably supernatural. Some years ago, when reviewing a book in the *Tablet*, I mentioned my own view of Ezechiel's dumbness, and since no one thought it worth while to contradict me, I venture to elaborate the suggestion here; as there is such a crop of unproven theories, one more—for what it is worth—is not likely to upset people.[1] I submit simply that Ezechiel's tongue-tied state was the well-understood form of contemplative prayer which is known as the 'ligature.'

Experience shows that at a certain stage in its spiritual course the soul finds that it cannot articulate properly; speech fails when apparently most needed. At the Divine

[1] To mention the opinions of only a few authorities, Kraetzschmar (*Das Buch Ezechiel*) advances the theory of epileptic fits. Buzy (*Les Symboles de l'Ancien Testament*) makes it paralysis and rheumatism. Holscher (*Die Propheten*) gives nervous exhaustion. Lods (*The Prophets and The Rise of Judaism*) suggests attacks of aphasia 'when gesture was the only means of expression.' So even if we judge the matter on purely *natural* grounds, there is a fairly wide field of investigation.

Office, for example, or when reciting any prayers out loud, the lips are unable to frame the words, and the only alternatives are to babble or keep quiet. The state is by no means uncommon. Much the same thing is liable to happen when preaching. Any exercise, in fact, which moves the soul to a profound appreciation of God's presence within it is quite likely to rob the speaking faculty of coherent expression. Père Poulain, in his great work on mysticism, *Graces of Interior Prayer*, has a passage which might almost have been written as a commentary on this second chapter of Ezechiel. 'The word *ligature*,' writes Père Poulain, 'indicates the condition of a man whose limbs are bound more or less tightly by bands, and who can only therefore move with difficulty.'[1] In the same section the writer goes on to say that 'in the prayer of quiet it [speech] does not amount to an absolute impossibility. Thus we can begin to recite a vocal prayer such as the Pater Noster, but after two or three words some unknown and secret force often stops us, and we hesitate and stammer. . . . The ligature is weak when the prayer of quiet is weak.'

A good illustration of a soul in this state of prayer might be cited from the autobiographical writings of Blessed Angela of Foligno. Our Lord spoke to the servant of God as follows: 'This sign I give to thee that I am He. Try now to speak with thy companions and think of other things, and thou wilt not be able to think of aught but God. For I am He alone Who can bind fast the mind.' We are further reminded of the account in Ezechiel when we read the sequel to the words just quoted. 'Thus, then, He withdrew,' Blessed Angela continues, 'nor did He permit me to fall down as He was leaving, but *I stood upon my feet*. Nevertheless after His departure I fell down in a

[1] p. 178.

sitting position, and began to cry with a loud voice and to
scream; and I cried out without any shame, calling aloud
and saying this word: "O my Love, hitherto I have not
known Thee, why dost Thou leave me thus?" But more
I could not say, except that in crying this out I wished to
form the word and say it *and I could not form it*, so wrapped
up it was in my voice and cry; and the word was not
understood by them that heard. Now this cry and ex-
clamation happened unto me at the entrance of the door
of the church of St. Francis, where, after the departure of
God I sat languishing; and I cried aloud and called out
in the presence of all the people, insomuch that they who
had come with me stood afar off and were ashamed,
believing that there was some other cause for it. *Our
Lord left me therefore with the certainty that He Who had spoken
to me was God.* Moreover by reason of His sweetness and
for sorrow at His departure, I cried out and wished to die;
and great was my grief that I did not die, and that I remained when He was gone. And at that moment all my
limbs were disjointed. And after this I went back from
Assisi. And with great sweetness I went along the way
speaking of God. *And it was to me the greatest punishment to
be silent.* [1]

Blessed Angela's case illustrates only one aspect of the
ligature—the prayer aspect; the limitation which it
imposes in a slightly different direction—the preaching
direction—is as well illustrated by the experience of the
celebrated Dominican preacher, John Tauler. The sudden
and intense recollection with which this friar was visited
at the beginning of one of his sermons was so overwhelming
that he was obliged to leave the pulpit. It seems that the
voice, the words, and even the thoughts escape control
when the touch of God is felt upon the soul, and, to the

---

[1] *The Book of the Visions and Instructions of Blessed Angela of Foligno*, ch. xx.
The words in italics—intended to show the likeness between Blessed Angela
and Ezechiel—are of course mine.

extreme embarrassment and mortification of the re-
cipient of these graces, the thing is noticed by other people.
Souls of prayer are very often puzzled and upset when
they find themselves in this state. God does not always—
as He did in the cases of Ezechiel and Angela and others—
proclaim the fact that it is He who is binding the faculties.
But there is no earthly need to be worried; the ligature
is not as purposeless as it seems; it is merely a necessary
working out of a perfectly straightforward law. It is the
law of spiritual distribution: you can't go on receiving
strictly supernatural favours with strictly natural faculties—something is bound to feel the strain. And in the
case of the ligature it is the speech which is wrapped up
for a time: its natural energy must not be allowed to
interfere with what is going on within.

It is, then, at least arguable that Ezechiel's dumbness
was due to the state of prayer above described. How far
does this answer our original questions? First, his impotence *does* seem to have been intended—if not in a
primary, at least in a secondary way—to correct any over-
confidence or self-congratulation which might come up in
Ezechiel's work of preaching. Second, it need not (as I
understand it) have affected the prophet's *un*prophetical
life. Outside the strictly spiritual sphere, a soul at this
stage of contemplative prayer may be, though not always
is, just like anybody else.[1] I say 'may be' because some

[1] So presumably Ezechiel could have answered ordinary questions and
issued ordinary instructions in a perfectly ordinary tone of voice. We can
return to Père Poulain for the justification of this. 'Let us examine the acts
with regard to which this impediment is felt. They are those that I have
previously called *additional acts*. Further it is only a question of voluntary
acts, such as the recitation of a vocal prayer.' I take it that the writer means
by 'voluntary' acts *any* act in which the will is brought into play—whether
the act is 'of obligation' (such as the Divine Office for a priest and religious)
or purely voluntary in the non-technical sense (as would be the Rosary).
The point is that the ligature is likely to affect all forms of *praise*—whether
in the choir-stall, the pulpit or the cell. It does not necessarily make praise
impossible (unless the ligature gives place to 'suspension') but it makes it
exceedingly difficult. It has to. Otherwise the soul would not be quiet
enough to practise the prayer it is meant to be practising—namely the
prayer of quiet. Not the finished prayer of quiet perhaps (which involves
suspension), but at least the beginnings of it.

are quite definitely not.   St. Catherine de Ricci, for example, was so abstracted by the generally stunning effect of her ligatures that she was looked upon for years as a sort of gentle lunatic.

It may be objected that if Ezechiel enjoyed this kind of prayer—a form of the prayer of quiet—how is it that he was constantly breaking into violent action? The answer would be that such is often an effect produced by that kind of prayer. This is not the place to discuss *why* so contradictory a symptom should manifest itself, suffice it to say merely that such a symptom is in no way contradictory. It is surely not extraordinary that energies which find their supernatural impulse in inward silence should find their natural expression in outward action. The brooding calm of the heavens (to borrow the imagery of the mystics) can throw off its thunderbolts . . . the fountain can spring up from the surface of the smoothest lake.

CHAPTER V

EZECHIEL ACTS

I

AND I mean 'acts.' Not merely takes action, but acts—performs. Speak he cannot; preach he must. So at the bidding of the Lord he acts.

> 'And thou, son of man, take thee a tile and lay it before thee, and draw upon it the city of Jerusalem. And lay a siege against it, and build forts, and cast up a mount, and set a camp about it and place battering rams round about it. And take unto thee an iron pan, and set it for a wall of iron between thee and the city; and set thy face resolutely against it, and it shall be besieged, and thou shalt lay siege against it. It is a sign to the house of Israel.'

This is the first of a series of symbolical acts. Some commentators hold that the prophet performed none of them. Ezechiel, they tell us, being primarily a literary prophet, was simply making use of a literary artifice.[1] But as there seems no earthly point in his talking about them if they did not happen, we will assume that the 'signs' were actually performed; a serious-minded prophet of the Lord would hardly have wanted to puzzle future generations of readers—not to mention readers of his own generation who, in far away Jerusalem, had no running commentaries to help them—merely for the sake of a literary flourish.

The prophet was told, then, to get hold of a tile or brick, and make a sort of relief map of its surface. In the vicinity of Babylon there would have been any amount of these soft asphalt bricks lying about; the capital was mostly built of them. In fact, the land of the Chaldeans

---

[1] 'The symbols stood actually before his imagination, and the narration of them to the people would convey the same instruction as the actual representation of them.' Davidson, *op. cit.* p. 30.

was reputed for its brick-kilns, traces of which can be seen today. Nearly all Nabuchodonosor's building enterprises were carried out in this medium, and we can judge from the specimens of his bricks which are preserved in the British Museum what a very serviceable material it was. For structural purposes and for decorative effect the brick is hard to beat. Nabuchodonosor's palace—basement, walls, vaulting and all—was entirely brick; so was the Ishtar Gate with its glazed façade; so also were the vast defences of the city—keeps, walls, buttresses and the rest.[1] For Ezechiel to use as a writing pad one of these bricks before it had properly hardened would have been the obvious thing to do; historical records and family archives were committed to bricks and tiles. The 'cylinders' which filled the libraries of Mesopotamia were only bricks with their corners rounded off and rolled into the shape of a fat cigar; for the preservation of Babylonia's history we owe as much to the durable quality of the composition of these cylinders as we do to the penmanship of the archivists who wrote upon them.

So Ezechiel seems to have fingered a cake of this clay-like substance into a more or less recognisable model of

[1] 'Among the most interesting things to be seen in Babylon are bricks still stuck together with asphalt instead of mortar, exactly as Herodotus described them. He was in Babylon about a century after its fall, when it was still the greatest city in the world although some of the buildings had been torn down. Possibly the punishment it had received from Xerxes gave the builders plenty to do, so that Herodotus may often have watched the asphalt gangs at work with their trolleys of burning pitch. The method of building was to lay a thin film of hot asphalt between each row of bricks; and bricks cemented in this way are so firm that they have to be broken apart with a pickaxe. Every now and then a layer of reeds would be inserted, and you can see their clear impression in the asphalt, in the places where the reeds have rotted away. Supplies of asphalt were available, says Herodotus, at Hit, about seventy miles west-north-west of Baghdad, a town which even today smells horribly of sulphuretted hydrogen, and has two asphalt wells, one hot and the other cold, within thirty feet of one another. . . . In ancient times writers from the West were invariably surprised and interested by the bricks and asphalt, which they regarded as a Babylonian characteristic, as indeed it was. The Tower of Babel was constructed of mud and brick and asphalt. . . .' Morton, *Through Lands of The Bible*, p. 70.

Jerusalem. We can easily imagine the scene. Perhaps he did not know, when he left his house that morning, that his sermon was to be acted and not spoken. Perhaps he had already gathered a crowd round him with the intention of thundering out some terrible threat with a voice as nearly as possible resembling Jeremias's, when, as had frequently happened lately, his tongue seemed to be getting in the way of his words. We can hear the opening phrases of his discourse trailing away into a burble of incoherences. We can see the amused interest of the audience, the embarrassment of the preacher, the anxious looks of the few devoted friends. But against the outward confusion of the central figure is balanced a great inward ordering of ideas. Whatever has happened to Ezechiel's words, 'the Word of God is not bound.'[1] The prophet of the Lord sees in a flash what is wanted of him. A brick, fetch me a brick . . . and a few minutes later a celebrated orator is seen making his first amateurish efforts in the world of plastic art.

II

That blob (so is the correct guess of a bystander) represents the Temple; the thumbnail scratch must be the brook of Kedron; the cone-shaped thing at the side would be Mount Olivet.

The artist looks up. He is wondering (so is the whispered information—again correct) if we are all here, and paying attention.

The model is raised and exhibited. Everyone seen it? Right. It is lowered again on to the prophet's lap, and, with a few deft strokes, alterations are made to the design. While you wait there appear round the edge of the tile a number of little mounds which bring a quite new character to the object lesson. The lumps assume detail. You see what they are (continues, quite correctly, the

[1] 2 Timothy 11, 9.

knowledgeable bystander): they are forts and battering rams and ramparts and things.

And then the word goes round: 'The Holy City is being besieged.'

All this may seem to us rather childish and laboured. The truth is we are too sophisticated. It is the saints—and sometimes the savants—who are big enough to play with toys. And it needs a people which understands sanctity to understand the seriousness of a pantomime—especially if the pantomime be a mystery play. The Jews, for all their infidelity, possessed a certain spiritual awareness which allowed them to follow the language of prophecy—even if the prophecy was expressed in plasticine. Ezechiel's subsequent behaviour was to teach the people of Tel-Abib that this was the kind of thing they were to expect from the choked-up mouthpiece of the Lord. The present pantomime was to have many variations in the future; the present *motif*—Jerusalem threatened from without—would become as familiar, and as unheeded, as the call to prayer. In different mimings Ezechiel would express God's warning; with different excuses the Jews would put off the thought of doom.

III

From the tile demonstration Ezechiel went straight on to enact another. Symbolising the blockade of Jerusalem, he placed a sheet of iron between himself and the model which he had just made. From an erect posture he altered his act by lying down. It speaks well for the intelligence of his crowd that all this was understood; most of us would have had to do some quick thinking in order to see what was the point of such apparently meaningless gestures. The significance lay, it seems, in the fact that the siege itself was no longer the main consideration, but rather that it was to the people within the city, the besieged, that attention was now being drawn. Ezechiel remained prostrate on the ground to show the powerlessness of the Jews under the scourge. For a time he leaned on his left side and for a time on his right: the left was to indicate Israel's prostration, the right was to indicate Juda's. And if it be asked how the people in Tel-Abib could possibly have read this meaning into the prophet's action, the only answer one can give is that one has not the least idea.

IV

Immediately after the above comes this:

'Take to thee,' says the Lord to Ezechiel, 'wheat and barley and beans and lentils and millet and fitches, and put them in one vessel, and make thee bread thereof according to the number of the days thou shalt lie upon thy side: three hundred and ninety days shalt thou eat thereof . . . from time to time thou shalt eat it. And thou shalt drink water by measure, the sixth part of a hin; from time to time thou shalt drink it.'

The act symbolises first the scarcity which will attend the siege, and second the ceremonial uncleanness which will be incurred by eating of a mixture made from different kinds of grain. This latter prophecy of pollution is further emphasised by the Lord's instruction (in verse 12) to mingle dung with the concoction of wheat and barley and beans. That famine and pollution did, as a fact, attend the siege of Jerusalem is certain from the account which we get from the Books of Jeremias and Lamentations. Ezechiel's answer to the above injunctions is worth noticing: it is almost word for word what St. Peter said to God when he was told to eat the 'creeping things' at Joppe. 'Ah, ah, ah, Lord God,' was Ezechiel's observation, 'Behold my soul hath not been defiled, and from my infancy even until now I have not eaten anything that died of itself or was torn by beasts, and no unclean flesh hath entered into my mouth.' One feels that this

verse must have escaped St. Peter's notice or he would
hardly have made the same excuse for refusing what was
being offered him; with the Ezechiel incident behind him
he would have known that it was useless to try and get
out of the business on such a plea. Ezechiel was told quite
simply to do what he was told: 'Thou shalt make thy
bread,' said God, 'therewith.' Which ended it.

V

Another of the prophet's demonstrations is described in
the chapter following. This time the appeal is in a somewhat lighter key; one senses an exuberance about this
next performance which is lacking in most of his others;
one hopes that this is the Ezechiel of private life. He gives
himself a public hair-cut. However successful or un-
successful he may have been with grown up Israel, he
must surely have been welcomed with enthusiasm by the
children—especially since for this hair-cut of his he used
a sword.

Having shaved his head and beard, Ezechiel was interiorly instructed to gather together the hair and weigh
it in a balance.

> 'A third part thou shalt burn with fire in the
> midst of the city, according to the fulfilling of the
> days of the siege; and thou shalt take a third part
> and cut it in pieces with the sword all round about;
> and the other third part thou shalt scatter in the
> wind, and I will draw out the sword after them. And
> thou shalt take thereof a small number, and shalt
> bind them in the skirt of thy cloak. And thou shalt
> take of them again, and shalt cast them in the midst of
> the fire, and shalt burn them with fire; and out of it
> shall come forth fire unto all the house of Israel.'

What looks like a conjuring trick of a highly elaborate
kind is really a one-piece morality play. The explanation is as follows : As hair which belongs to the head is

removed by a sharp instrument, so Juda which belongs to the Holy City will be cut off by the sword from its natural habitation. The severed race will then be divided into three parts: a third to be burned, a third to be smitten by the sword, a third to be scattered to the winds; of these, the last group, a remnant will be scraped together, and then another partitioning will take place; some to suffer famine and burning, some to escape 'yet so as by fire.'

This must have given Tel-Abib something to think about. And for those who were not inclined to think it must at least have given something to remember. What a sight to recall in later years! A mute prophet lashing about with a sword . . . great hanks of hair flying in all directions . . . the business with the scales . . . the miniature bonfire . . . the flinging of the ashes to the winds of heaven. And the ominous silence of the prophet must have made the performance far more impressive than any amount of ranting would have done; the miming of a mummer is a far more sinister thing than the wailings of a witch or the screamings of a skeleton.

Hair assumes a significance in the Old Testament which we, in an almost beardless generation, perhaps find puzzling. The Nazarite vow, for example, forbad the use of the razor; and to the Hebrew mind the action of Ezechiel—even though the prophet was not a Nazarite—would have seemed distinctly daring. The Hebrews had been taught to value hair, and to regard it even with a sort of reverence: Samson relied on it for supernatural strength,[1] Solomon sang in praise of it,[2] Judith adorned it,[3] mourning was expressed by the removal of it, insults were conveyed by the removal of half of it,[4] and Eliseus was laughed at for not having it.[5]

[1] Judges xvi.
[2] Canticles v, 11.
[3] Judith x, 3.
[4] 2 Kings x, 4.
[5] 4 Kings ii, 23.

VI

'Can you see what's going on?' a voice is asking on the fringe of the crowd. 'No, I'm afraid I can't,' is the answer, 'but from what one knows of Ezechiel, he's not likely to let us miss much; the obvious thing is to wait.' They wait. A thin coil of smoke is seen over the heads of the people in front, and there is a faint smell of singed hair. A new kind of holocaust? Burning his prayer mat? 'Could you hoist me up for a moment? Thank you.' And the crowd in the market-place silently contemplates the spectacle of its spiritual leader fanning with his hand a reluctant and uncertain flame. Tufts of hair curl and sizzle and then crumble into grey ash. . . . Jerusalem, Jerusalem, be thou converted unto the Lord thy God.

CHAPTER VI

MORE MYSTICAL EXPERIENCES

I

WITH the sixth chapter of the Prophecy Ezechiel introduces a new division of the Book. We hear now what the prophet has to say about Juda's threefold sin—apostasy, idolatry and hardness of heart—and how he warns his hearers of the evils which must come in punishment. If these chapters were given to the public in written form there is no difficulty; if they were spoken, however, we must make allowance for a period of respite in the divinely imposed silence. In point of fact, the indications seem in any case to suggest that this was a portion of the Prophecy which was written down and never actually delivered by word of mouth. The sixth and seventh chapters are a dirge over Juda's downfall; the eighth, ninth and tenth describe a vision which illustrates this downfall; the eleventh holds out the remedy; the twelfth begins all over again to tell of Jerusalem's collapse. Leaving out the lament contained in chapters six and seven, we can devote a short chapter to the horrors which the prophet saw mystically enacted in the Holy City and in the Temple. It is a depressing interlude.

'And it came to pass in the sixth year, in the sixth month, in the fifth day of the month, as I sat in my house and the ancients of Juda sat before me, that the hand of the Lord fell upon me.'

Before we examine the vision which followed, it would be as well to observe again the prophet's exactitude in the matter of dates; the mention of the 'elders' seems even to imply that if anyone doubted his accuracy there were witnesses alive who would bear him out. Now who were these elders? Perhaps they were men who had enjoyed some sort of official position at home and who were now honoured with a courtesy title. Possibly the community at Tel-Abib was, after all, allowed to elect a quasi governing body, and perhaps these men represented it. Whoever they were and whether recognised by Babylon or not, these elders evidently saw in Ezechiel the true mouthpiece of the Lord, and, from time to time, were willing to consult him on matters of religion. Though they may have objected to his behaviour and shrunk from the implications of his teaching, they would have felt bound—and in fact did feel bound—to respect the traditional priesthood; they may even have belonged to it themselves.

I have suggested that the ancients came to consult Ezechiel about religion; the reason why it seems to have been religion (rather than politics or art or social welfare or market-gardening or any of the hundred and one other things it might have been) is simply that it produced a peculiar effect—it brought on an ecstasy. Which, if Ezechiel's affliction was what we have supposed it to be, is just what we would expect it to do. Pretty well anything which brought God, or the things of God, forcibly before the mind would have been likely to precipitate one of Ezechiel's profound abstractions, but a deputation, coming as it did from the leaders of Juda's religious life and taking place in his own house—probably in his oratory and at a time when he was accustomed to pray anyway—would certainly have increased the chances of something rather violent taking place in his soul. Added to this, of course, it was the will of the Lord just then to communicate something to His servant's soul.

So no sooner were the spokesmen of God's people settled down before the spokesman of God's word than Ezechiel was wrapt away with the vehemence of his prayer. The same sort of thing used to happen to St. Teresa when her nuns or St. John of the Cross would come to speak to her of the love of God.

'And the likeness of a hand was put forth and took me by a lock of my head, and the spirit lifted me up between the earth and the heaven, and brought me in the vision of God to Jerusalem near the inner gate that looked toward the north, where was set the idol of jealousy in the very entry.'

The rest of the chapter is taken up with the evils which his vision showed him—evils which were practised in various parts of the Temple and by every condition of men. The passage gives us a fearful catalogue of crime and double living; even the reputed leaders of Israel are accounted guilty, seventy of them burning the incense of idol worship, and among that number Jezonias the son of devout Saphan the scribe. Of all the horrors mentioned in this part of Ezechiel's Book there is something peculiarly horrible about the presence of Jezonias among the idolators. There is irony in the thought that just as Saphan had been one of the prime movers in the restoration of true worship during the last generation, so his son was a ringleader of false worship in this. Almost deliberately the Bible seems to give the same setting to father and to son: the 'composition of place' is in each case the Temple. One man honours, the other desecrates. *Corruptio optimi pessima.*

'Therefore I will deal with them in My wrath. My eye shall not spare them, neither will I show them mercy. And when they shall cry to My ears with a loud voice I will not hear them.'

So ends this terrible chapter.

II

We have touched briefly on what God's people have done to God; we must examine closer what God will do to His people. The threat contained in the last quoted verse is, in the same vision, seen fulfilled. The text as we have it is somewhat unwieldy, so we shall not miss much if we confine ourselves to a summary. The full account is contained in the prophet's ninth chapter.

Ezechiel saw six men, officers of state, coming towards him; in the hand of each was a weapon of destruction. A seventh man, clothed in a linen alb and carrying an ink-horn at his waist, then appeared in the midst of them. The full company proceeded to the brazen altar, and there stood awaiting instructions from the Lord. The man who was clothed in linen was then called upon by 'the Glory of the Lord' to go through the city of Jerusalem and write the Hebrew letter Tau upon the foreheads of all who were mourning over the outrages done in the Temple. Apart from those thus signed, every man, woman, and child would have to suffer at the hands of the six armed companions. This slaughter was to begin at the Temple itself; where the Lord had been most blasphemed, there would his vengeance be most fully manifest. 'And they went forth,' Ezechiel tells us, 'and smote the city.' We can pause here before examining the effect which this had upon the poor tortured soul who watched first his city's shame and then its spoliation.

III

A word, to begin with, upon this letter Tau. St. Jerome, with a whole host of later writers, sees in the sign of Tau the sign of Christ's Cross. The sign which is to appear in the clouds on the last day, the sign which is made on our foreheads at Baptism, the sign which blesses our work, our food, our sleep, and the sign which is the last sign to be made over us before our dead bodies are hidden from the light of day, is also, by one of those divinely planned coincidences which we often meet in Sacred Scripture, the sign whereby the remnant will be saved. Even in the Old Testament the Passion is never very far away; if the prophets are not foretelling it, and if the types of Christ—such as David, Joseph, Jonas and others— are not in their very lives foreshadowing it, there are significant hints every now and again which point to it. The serpent of Moses which was raised aloft in the desert to stay the plague is one such thing.[1] The recurring sign of Tau is another.[2] It is as if whenever there is a question

---

[1] Numbers xxi, 9.   [2] cf. Exodus xii, 7.

of man being saved in the face of almost certain doom, the sacred writer of the moment is caused to point, perhaps unconsciously, to the grounds of all salvation. Whatever the Hebrew character meant in its further applications to the prophet Ezechiel, its sacred import was perfectly recognised by St. John.[1] Warned of the Cross in the Old Testament, shown it by the Crucified Himself in the New, receiving in its name the Sacraments of Christ's Church, can there be any excuse for us if we be unfamiliar with its implications? Ashamed shall we be indeed if, when the great day comes and the Cross—as cross-roads must— marks the parting of the ways, we are found to have worn the sign of Christ's Redemption as a badge merely and not as the expression of our love.

IV

To show that the general devastation which was promised in the vision was no idle threat, we can point to the Second Book of Paralipomenon, and trace the history of those ravaging weeks. The chronicler, having told how the people of God had 'mocked the messengers of God and misused the prophets,' relates in graphic terms the sack of the Holy City. 'The Lord brought upon them the king of the Chaldeans,' he says, 'and slew their young men in the house of His sanctuary, and He had no compassion on young man or maiden, old man or even him that stooped for age, but He delivered them all into his hands. And the vessels of the house of the Lord, great and small, and the treasures of the Temple and of the king and of the princes he carried away to Babylon.'[2] But there is this important little addition which shows that the slaying was not extended to every living Jew: 'Whosoever escaped the sword was led away. . . .' While there is yet a handful, there is yet a hope. One of the things which impresses us in reading Scripture is this constant alternation between trustful buoyancy on the

[1] Apocalypse vii, 3.   [2] 2 Paralipomenon xxxvi, 16, 17, 18.

one hand and very nearly desperation on the other. It is
not even as if one prophet were raised up to preach about
the sunshine and another to preach about the shadow, it is
rather that each prophet is raised up to preach about both.
And if we, reading the Old Testament, feel that we are
being swept from light to shade and from shade back again
to light, it is comforting to think that even some of the
sacred writers themselves felt the same when they turned
the pages of their predecessors. Surely St. Peter had been
reading Ezechiel when, within a few verses of each other,
he wrote down the following thoughts: 'The time is that
judgement should begin at the house of God. And if first
at us, what shall be the end of them that believe not the
gospel of God? . . . 'And when the Prince of pastors shall
appear, you shall receive a never-fading crown of glory.'[1]
And in his Second Epistle: 'But the day of the Lord shall
come as a thief, in which the heavens shall pass away with
great violence . . .' while at the same time we have reason
to 'look for and hasten unto the coming of the day of the
Lord . . . looking for new heavens and a new earth according to His promises in which justice dwelleth.'[2] To
the sons of God, then, hope is never wholly deferred, and
fear never wholly stifled: the soul is kept in the balance
under the mighty hand of God.

V

To return to Ezechiel's vision:

> 'And the slaughter being ended I was left. And
> I fell upon my face, and crying I said: Alas, alas,
> alas, O Lord God, wilt thou then destroy all the
> remnant of Israel by pouring out Thy fury upon
> Jerusalem? And He said to me: the iniquity of the
> house of Israel and of Juda is exceeding great, and
> the land is filled with blood, and the city is filled with
> perverseness . . . therefore I will requite their way
> upon their head. And behold the man that was

[1] 1 Peter iv, 17; v, 4.   [2] 2 Peter iii, 10, 13.

clothed in linen and that had the ink-horn at his back returned the word saying: I have done as Thou hast commanded me.'

So it seems that the horror of what he saw coming upon Jerusalem drove out of Ezechiel's heart the resentment which he had been feeling against God's rebellious children. The prophet was appalled, and took upon himself the unexpected office of advocate. True, his efforts came to nothing, but we must keep in mind the fact that he made them: only too often do we see a picture of what seems to be a ruthless Ezechiel, so it is as well that we should retain a picture of a tender one. The prophet made a second attempt at mediation in the next chapter but one,[1] and this time he was successful—or at all events, partly successful.

Still in the vision, God had added to the scourges above described a rain of fire from the heavens. The prophet had been placed by the Spirit upon a pinacle of the eastern gate of the Temple, and from here he was told to look down at the men who had 'devised iniquity,' and to denounce them. This he did, and when he saw how immediate was the effect of his denunciation ('it came to pass when I prophesied that Pheltias the son of Babaias died'), he fell prostrate before the Lord and repeated his prayer for mercy. Whereupon the Lord revealed His plan. In effect the will of God amounted to this, that though the capital was to be wiped out, Israel would ultimately revive.

Jerusalem had sinned, Jerusalem must suffer; and so those who had left Jerusalem and who had not sinned (that is, the faithful Jews of the Captivity) would in future be regarded as the only true spiritual citizens of Jerusalem. The Jews at home had shown themselves unworthy: very well, it was now time to concentrate upon the dispersed—perhaps *they* would live according to their call. All this Ezechiel was instructed to declare to the people.

[1] xi.

What it must have cost him to do so! He, the nationalist, the Zionist, the priest. His function to tell his fellow Jews that Jerusalem was not so all-important to the working out of God's plan after all. Would men understand him when he told them that there was a refuge more sure than any they should find on Sion? Would men ever leave their sheltering city walls for the still more sheltering arms of God? Deprived of a Temple made with hands the true Jews must henceforth dwell in the temples of their souls. 'And I saw no Temple therein,' says St. John of the New Jerusalem, 'for the Lord God Almighty is the Temple thereof, and the Lamb. And the city hath no need of the sun nor of the moon to shine in it. For the Glory of the Lord hath enlightened it, and the Lamb is the lamp thereof.'[1]

Yes, St. John and Ezechiel might talk about their New Jerusalems because it was given them to see the future as they prayed. But how about the rest, the men of Israel, to whom the Old Jerusalem was all in all? Well, they must be taught to live by faith and not by sight. They must be trained to see that though the heart seem to fall right out of the body, *on that account* would God substitute His own Heart . . . to see that eventually, in God's good time, the severed veins of Juda would reunite and find their life-stream in Him.

'Therefore,' says the Lord to Ezechiel, 'speak to them: Thus saith the Lord God: I will gather you from among the peoples, and assemble you out of the countries wherein you are scattered, and I will give you the land of Israel . . . and I will give them one heart, and will put a new spirit within them; and I will take away the stony heart out of their flesh, and will give to them a heart of flesh . . . that they may be My people and I may be their God.'

The intimacy of it! Almost the *anxiety* of it—the divine desire for closer union with His people! Was there ever a

[1] Apocalypse xxi, 22, 23.

sweeter invitation than that which is contained in the assurance that 'I will give to them a heart of flesh'? A heart which will at last do what hearts are made for doing: a heart which will love back.

And then, to round off the narrative of this extra-ordinary vision, we have this verse: 'The Glory of the Lord went up from the midst of the city, and stood over the mount that is on the east side of the city . . . and the vision which I had seen was lifted from me.' See where the Glory of the Lord went to—it went to the Mount of Olives. Fitting indeed that the vision of God's Glory should fade where the reality of God's Passion began. Olivet's tragedy is foreshadowed by the brooding of the Spirit over the apostate city of Jerusalem.

VI

One wonders if the elders were still waiting when Eze-chiel came out of his ecstasy; we are told nothing of what they thought or said about 'all the words of the Lord which He had shown' to His servant. Did they doubt the orthodoxy of the experience? Did they claim to interpret its import? Did they comment on the prophet's delivery of the message—twisting it to suit the policies or the philosophies or the prejudices of the moment? These ancients, for all we know, may have been sympathetic; but somehow one fancies not. They will appear again later on—also under the suspicion of sceptical enquiry. One thing of which we may be pretty sure is that when these grave, official, practical, respectable men of affairs sat in conclave to discuss the results of their deputation there was much talk of keeping one's head, of not taking things too literally, of looking at the past and seeing how even the most *difficult* situations had managed to solve themselves if one only waited and went about things quietly. . . .

'And I spoke to them of the captivity all the words of the Lord which He had shown me.' *All* the words. So there was no excuse.

CHAPTER VII

MORE SIGNS

I

If we may judge from the prophet's next recorded demonstrations, his message from God did, as a fact, fall upon deaf ears. If Tel-Abib did not actually reject the appeal out of hand, at least it hesitated to meet the implications: it did no penance. The children of Israel had heard this kind of thing before, but the storm clouds of Jehovah's wrath had invariably given place to the blue sky of His favour; again and again He had proved Himself most anxious to preserve His people. He would doubtless continue in this course. So why bother? Besides which, Ezechiel was not the only prophet in the pulpit, and others—less ardent spirits perhaps, but none the less bearing certain vague claims to authenticity—had predicted no such calamities.[1]

At all events, both the dispersed at Tel-Abib and the Jews at home allowed themselves, when they learned of what we have treated in the foregoing chapter, a splendid unconcern. But Ezechiel's fire was not to be so easily quenched: where he had hitherto revealed the character of Israel's impending doom he would now reveal how imperative was its necessity.

'And the word of the Lord came to me saying: Son of man, thou dwellest in the midst of a provoking house, who have eyes to see and see not, and ears to hear and hear not; for they are a provoking house. Thou therefore, O son of man, prepare

[1] We shall find Ezechiel attacking these false mystics in ch. xiii. Jeremias had the same trouble from men who were for ever calling out the 'the Lord saith' this and that. In the ordinary way it might not have mattered much if a few deluded, or even deluding, souls had preached a private error or raised a little band of fanatics. But here the thing was more serious: the false prophets confirmed the exiles in their delusive expectations of a speedy return to a prosperous Jerusalem.

58

thee all necessaries for removing, and remove by day in their sight.'

The ensuing episode, of which this is the introduction, follows upon what has gone before without a break, so we can assume from what we know of the writer's care for dates and method that the interval between this and the vision described in the previous chapter was negligible. Promulgated visions do no good? All right, then, more signs.

Again the scene is the market place; again the busy, materially-minded and somewhat hostile throng; again the silent, gesticulating, desperately sincere prophet; again the absorbed and excited interest of the very young. This time the properties of Ezechiel's dumb-show seem to have included most of his movable possessions; he was also to require for his demonstration a wall and a quantity of loose earth.

Acting, then, on the verbal command of God, Ezechiel collected into what must have been a very unwieldy bundle such belongings as a man would take with him in a sudden evacuation from home. The bundle must have been considerable because we read of the Lord telling him to 'bring forth thy furniture, as the furniture of one that is removing.' All this had to be deposited, in the full light of day, at some spot which would not escape the observation of his fellow exiles. Standing beside the pile of clothes, bedding, cooking utensils, mats and sermon notes, Ezechiel would have waited for his cue. The audience provided it. 'So he's going away at last,' was the kind of comment he was expecting, and, having heard it, he picked up from the heap beside him all that he could conveniently carry on his back, and, with every appearance of furtive haste, made off in an easterly direction. 'In fact it looks more as if he's escaping than just moving,' was the next thing he wanted from his public. He got it. The Jews decided—just as any other crowd would have

done—to follow the fugitive prophet and see what he
would do next. The procession had not far to go before it
came to a halt. Instead of passing out of Tel-Abib by
the ordinary gateway, Ezechiel made straight for the city
wall (or for what corresponded to the city wall; Tel-
Abib would hardly have been a 'fenced city' with its
sheltering fortifications, but it probably had some sort of
mural boundary). Here, unless it was already evening by
this time, the crowd had to wait; we are distinctly told
that the next act was one which took place in the dark.

> 'And in the evening I digged through the wall
> with my hand, and I went forth in the dark, and I
> was carried on men's shoulders in their sight.'

The scene which this conjures up is dramatic indeed.
The feverish burrowing while the last glow of a quick
eastern twilight softens the outlines of the actor and his
audience . . . the hush which comes down upon them all
when they see that the work is finished and are waiting
for the next move . . . the flutter of loose garments as the
chill night breeze blows over the table-land of Chaldea. . . .
If only we knew more! We would like to know if there
was present the entire company of exiles, if the children
were allowed to stay up to see the end of it or were made
to go home to bed, if the 'elders' who had approached
Ezechiel shortly before were pleased or apprehensive—
or what? It seems likely that whatever the number of
venturesome souls who left their marketing to witness
Ezechiel's acting, a quite considerable mob would have
assembled to watch the tampering, on the part of an
'exile' and an 'alien,' with property belonging to the State.
You can't dig holes in other countries' walls without
being either applauded or arrested. It strikes us as curious
that Ezechiel was not stopped by the authorities before
he had got half through. Perhaps the Chaldean keepers
of the peace knew their man; perhaps the prophet was
preserved from interrupting by some judicious bribing on

the part of a few faithful friends; perhaps the whole
demonstration was performed with such despatch as
to escape official notice.[1]   What strikes us as possibly
more curious still is the reference to his being 'carried on
men's shoulders.'   It is only our version which has this
reading; other texts have 'I bare it upon my shoulder in
their sight'— referring to the bundle of belongings
which he had taken with him originally.   If this last is
right then there is no difficulty; if the Vulgate is right, then
there is the problem as to why on earth a proportion of the
male members of a presumably unsympathetic audience
should be found to assist in the performance to the extent
of bearing the central figure shoulder high.   It is only a
small point, of course, and in no way affects the course of
events, but I merely suggest that if our version *is* the
correct one, a possible solution may be found in—again—
the prophet's state of prayer.   In other words, that by the
time Ezechiel had come to the climax of what the Lord
had required of him to do, he lost control of his prayer
altogether, and became, as so many of the mystics have
become, incapable of movement and to outward appearance entirely unconscious.   If this *was* the case, then it
would have been necessary for some of those present to
carry him away.

'The word of the Lord came to me in the morning,
saying,' etc.   Thus the explanation is deferred to another
assembly.   This seems to bear out the above speculation.
Next day, when I had come round from my trance (is
the possible implication) I was enabled by God to give
the key to my mysterious action of the night before; the
people were so puzzled by the whole thing that God
lifted the ban of silence for the time being, and I was
able verbally to show the meaning of each symbolical act.

In the morning, then, what the Lord said to Ezechiel
was this:

[1] You can do a lot of damage to a mud wall in a comparatively short
time. It is odd, though, that Ezechiel had to use his hands and not a spade.

'Son of man, hath not the house of Israel, the provoking house, said to thee: What art thou doing? Say to them, therefore, Thus saith the Lord God: This burden concerneth My prince that is in Jerusalem and all the house of Israel that is among them. Say: I am a sign of things to come to you. As I have done so shall it be done to them: they shall be removed from their dwellings and shall go into captivity. And the prince that is in the midst of them shall be carried on shoulders [or, shall bear upon his shoulder], he shall go forth in the dark: they shall dig through the wall to bring him out; his face shall be covered that he may not see the ground with his eyes . . . and I will bring him into Babylon, into the land of the Chaldeans, and he shall not see it, and there he shall die.'

If yesterday Ezechiel's miming was received in a mixed spirit of entertainment and wonder, today—when in the morning the prophet makes his explanations—the prevailing sentiment must be one of awe. Here, in the place of obscure masquerades, was a perfectly clear statement— a statement which involved a definite person. When Jerusalem shall be taken (says the prophet), the king will try to escape; that was the meaning of my pretended flight. He will attempt to make his departure through a secret gap in the city wall; that was the reason for my furtive burrowing. He will fail in this, and his subsequent movements will be carried out in the dark . . . he will stumble over ground which he cannot see, he will live the rest of his life in exile at a place which shall be hidden from his eyes. He, Sedecias, king of Juda, will be blind.[1] Such was Ezechiel's key to yesterday's little drama. We have only to read 4 Kings xxv and Jeremias lii to see how

---

[1] It is worth noting that nowhere does Ezechiel refer to Sedecias as 'king'; the word he uses is always 'prince.' The reason for this is that Joachin was still alive, and, though an exile and prisoner in Babylon, was regarded by the nationalist Jews as the real king.

strictly all this was verified in the event. These things shall be signs, 'and they shall know that I am the Lord.'

One wonders how far the people saw into the heart of all this. They would certainly have followed the drift of Ezechiel's meaning—once the explanation had been given them—but what one would like to know is whether any of them saw a spiritual, even mystical, interpretation of Jerusalem's fall and Sedecias's fate. Did they apply the idea to the evacuation of their own souls—to that emptying of self which is necessary to the fulness of the indwelling of God? One likes to think that there were not wanting among the exiles at Tel-Abib men and women who were making it their whole business to lead the interior life, men and women who would have learned from their early training in the Holy City, and now from the direction of God's prophet, to follow the promptings of grace and to surrender themselves unconditionally to the unfolding of God's will. Unless, indeed, there were souls of this quality among the expatriated, the reverses of the last few years must surely have shaken the heart out of the race. Well then, would not these have seen a new meaning in the prophet's acts? Would they not have been reminded that for the Godward ascent to be successful *all* lesser things must be forgone? The soul must be swept of its natural affections however noble; of its natural perceptions however subtle; of its natural ambitions however worthy. Listen to St. John of the Cross: 'As long as the powers of the soul, which are like deeply hollowed caves, are not emptied and washed clean of all adherent creatures, they will not know how immensely deep is their capacity.'[1] The streets of Jerusalem are swept of its traffic and its crowds, but this is not enough; it is necessary that the first man in the realm should be ousted, should be made blind, should be carried away captive to another land. So also must the soul be freed of its traffic, must give up its treasures, must—saying good-

[1] *Living Flame*, III, 3.

bye to its natural activity—go out from itself into the in-
tellect's dark night; no longer even in the twilight of a
part comprehension, it must, in the blackness, stumble
over the uneven ground which leads to exile and captivity.
Only so can the full purpose of God be fulfilled, only so
can grace assert in the soul its unrestricted way. 'There is
but one means of winning to God,' is St. John's conclusion, 'and that way is this: to free the fettered spirit, to
make void the cumbered heart, to force the faculties to
renounce their normal overlordship and their natural
functioning that they may give place to the infused
illumination of the supernatural.'[1]   Sedecias's 'overlordship' was all too natural, and he had to go. God was
doing for Jerusalem what he has done for many a soul
since; fortunate are those souls who have no more say in
the matter than had Jerusalem. Shrinking from the hand
which leads us out from our native place we are ever in
danger of refusing the call to nakedness and exile. But
only so, in the darkness of faith, can we reach the final
goal of contemplation.

> *In a dark night,*
> *With anxious love inflamed,*
> *O happy lot!*
> *Forth unobserved I went,*
> *My house being now at rest.*
>
> *In that happy night,*
> *In secret, seen of none,*
> *Seeing nought myself,*
> *Without other light or guide*
> *Save that which in my heart was burning.*[1]

St. John's song is only an echo of Ezechiel's acted
canticle.   Both souls are tingling with the love that
drives them—the one to silent signs, the other to deathless

[1] *Ascent* III, i.   [1] *Dark Night*, stanzas 1 and 3.

verse. Their houses, emptied at long last by the twofold sweepings of sense and spirit, are now at rest. Unobserved they go out to the Beloved. O happy lot!

We ask again, did the men of Tel-Abib see under the skin of Ezechiel's deeds and words? Possibly not. Possibly they saw no more of the inwardness of prophecy than we, their descendants, see when we fail to take the trouble to look. Were we more 'with anxious love inflamed' it is possible that even such spiritual awareness as is ours would ripen into deeper penetration.

E—•

CHAPTER VIII

EZECHIEL VERSUS THE REST

I

EVEN after all that we have been considering in the last chapter the people *still* held back. 'But,' we can hear them saying, 'these things simply don't happen, my dear, so why worry.' And that other drug-phrase: 'Our children, poor things, will see great changes, but of course it's not the slightest use our doing anything.' So it is no surprise to us when we read of Ezechiel's return to the charge, or that the particular nature of his charge took the form of insisting that these things very definitely *did* happen, that they *were* worth worrying about, and that this present generation *would* be the victims of the changes he had threatened. And if the bogus prophets preached otherwise, then let it be known that Israel must choose between them and him. Which would Israel have—divination or revelation? The time had come for a decision: accept or reject, get in or get out.

'The days are at hand . . . not one word of Mine shall be prolonged any more . . . woe to the foolish prophets that follow their own spirit and see nothing . . . thy prophets, O Israel, are like foxes in the deserts.'

The 'fox' metaphor is a particularly happy one: it suggests the fatal influence, upon what is already crumbling, of fussy sniffing animals. Just as ruins are the hunting ground of the fox, so the tottering culture of Israel is a fair field to the charlatan; the fortune-teller can grub about to his heart's content in a religious observance which is running to seed.

Ezechiel made it his business, by means of cold scientific realism as well as by ardent oratory, to dissipate the mirage of false hope which all too long had been kept dancing before the tired eyes of the exiles at Tel-Abib.

'Peace, peace . . . there is no peace, saith the Lord.' As we read this tempestuous chapter of Ezechiel's we see how gloriously sure he was of his own authenticity and of his rivals' falsity; we see how entirely fearless he was in daring to attack the smooth-voiced illuminates whom he knew to have been more popular than himself. Sarcastically (surely) he allowed them the title 'prophet'. But he called them 'foolish' all the same. They were seers who saw nothing—nothing at all. Not even were they worldly wise: they were, in fact, worldly stupid—they could not boast of even human prudence. Had they possessed any sort of perception—political perception, let alone moral or spiritual perception—they would have hesitated before preaching a doctrine of national security. But of course these prophets had no insight into anything. So amateurish were their attempts at prophecy that even the terms they used were seen to have been borrowed from sources other than those of true revelation; their jargon was that of the soothsayers of Chaldea. The idiom of revealed Truth, then, was not good enough? The Word of Jehovah had been superseded by the catch-words of Chaldea? Witchcraft had come into its own, and prophecy had gone out from its own? Very well, then, there would never again be cause to mistake sorcery for prophecy—and this for the excellent reason that sorcery should cease.

> 'You shall not see'—even—'vain things, nor shall you divine divinations any more. I will deliver My people out of your hand; and you shall know that I am the Lord.'

II

But Ezechiel was to find himself in opposition to others besides false seers; the elders, whom we have met before and who seem in the interval to have hardened their hearts, were evidently proving themselves obstructionist. 'Obstructionist' is perhaps too thin a word for the conduct which is reproved by the Spirit in the Bible text:

> 'The ancients of Israel came to me and sat before me. And the word of the Lord came to me saying: Son of man, these men have placed their uncleannesses in their hearts, and have set up before their face the stumbling-block of iniquity; and shall I answer them when they enquire of Me?'

The message which Ezechiel now gave to the men in front of him is not very clear in the text, but the burden of it is roughly this: Don't come looking to me for oracular utterances. If you do what I say, I shall speak. But not otherwise. I'm not a fortune-teller. You pretend that you want my advice when what you really want is an insurance policy. My friends, you are sitting there with idols in your hearts. And it isn't good enough. Go away.

From the seventh to the twenty-third verse of this chapter we have proclaimed for us the miserable fate of the man, or race, that dares to compromise on the subject of true and false worship. The chapter which follows this continues the same thought; so also does chapter sixteen, which inclines us to suspect that the whole group of discourses was delivered at one sitting to the assembled elders. If this was so, the elders must have endured a longish harangue: Ezechiel seems to have made the most of the periods allowed him by God when speech came freely. By the time we have read to the end of chapter sixteen we find that the prophet has pitted himself against .pretty well every condition of Jew—the rich and poor, the pro-Egyptian and the pro-Chaldean, the older and the younger generation—'they have been transgressors, saith the Lord God.'

It would seem that the sad situation had by now arisen when the priest had despaired of his congregation and the congregation had despaired of its priest. Ezechiel could look forward only to a very far distant hope of his flock's return to God;[1] and the flock did not look forward at all. Commentators attribute the want of trust on the people's part to the enigmatical nature of the prophet's utterances. But surely this was not the reason. The Jews disliked their pastor, but it was not because they did not understand him; it was rather because they did. Crystal clear was the prophet's meaning, confused only was the sound of the prophet's words.

III

The elders got up and went. And just as we have been granted no account of what they said about the previous session, so now also the comments of these men are withheld from us. Were they the taciturn lot which, from what is left out in the Bible narrative, they seem to have been? We again look in vain for some sort of apologia, an objection or two, a mild heckle, a question. But no, they pass out of the prophet's chapter as silently as they came into his house.

When his guests have gone Ezechiel, praying in his oratory, tastes the bitter fruit of rejected service. More than ever does he feel himself cut off from his people. But he is not lonely in that abject sense of having none from whom he can expect understanding: he has God and he has his wife . . . he is content. A man can hardly fear to face his apostolate single-handed so long as he knows that he is being watched by those he loves. As far as his work goes, Ezechiel is alone; as far as his life goes, he is able to share it. No, he may not be lonely in the strict sense, but one does seem to see at this stage in the unfolding of his Prophecy a certain lull, a mental fatigue or even a purely physical reaction after strain, which suggests disappointment. Not bitterness—disappointment merely. The chapters which immediately follow are shot with the dyes of failure. Up till now the prophet has *done* things. They have not been very successful things,

[1] 60-63.

but he has energised over them; he has made his concrete contribution to God's service. From now on he will not be called upon so much to do things as to suffer them being done. He will, it is true, go on fighting, go on preaching, and even to a certain extent go on acting, but these will be only by-products, as it were, to the main industry of silent suffering and prayer. He is by no means through with his life's work—even his outward, active work—but he has arrived at a mile-stone, and, as people do when they arrive at mile-stones, he sits on it. 'All action in any direction,' says De Quincey,[1] 'is best expounded, measured, made apprehensible, by re-action,' and though the soul itself may seldom be granted to measure and apprehend the value either of what has gone before or the true quality of the 're-action,' yet we who come after can sometimes see success where nothing but flat failure was expounded at the time.

If Ezechiel was settling himself down to a period of inaction he was certainly not settling himself down to a period of fruitlessness: the characterisation which he went in for does not, in the supernatural order, depend for its merit on human audiences. Ezechiel's most fruitful act was his act of faith. It was the life of faith which he was now, more even than hitherto, called upon by Almighty God to live.

[1] Who, incidentally, knew his Ezechiel; he compares the prophet to the poet Æschylus.

CHAPTER IX

RIDDLES AND PARABLES

I

WITH chapter seventeen we have come to a section of the Prophecy which would seem to give colour to the theory which divides the honours of authorship between an accurate, date-recording, subsectioning, pigeon-holing Ezechiel on the one hand and a poetic, image-loving, carelessly-compiling Ezechiel on the other. So far we have mostly had the Ezechiel who writes with a diary propped up in front of him, now we shall find ourselves turning the pages of an Ezechiel who is looking out of the window most of the time. I hope to show in a later chapter of this book what the opening chapter has already suggested—that the Prophecy is a coat without seam, woven by the same hand throughout. Suffice to note here that the prophet's method changes though the prophet's mind abides. And the method changes, one ventures to think, because it has been found not to work very well.

It is one of the lessons which we learn from God's servants that they can keep their ideals and yet let go of their ways of approaching them. The purpose remains while the gang-planks—humanly devised and necessary enough to begin with—have suffered substantial alteration. With most of us the process is almost exactly the opposite. In the history of sanctity we find that true reformers, when they see one system to be a failure, are wise enough to apply another. The true reformer knows that you can alter theories and practices, but you cannot alter people; you can raise the ideals of people just as you can lower the ideals of people, but you cannot change the people themselves. The educational system, the political constitution, the religious rule—if it is going to be of any real use—must be woven round the body which it sets out to inform; it must not be clapped on from above. Somehow the ideal has to be kept, even if its interpretation

has to be scrapped. It is the function of the true leader
to decide upon what is to be retained and what is to be
rejected—what is of the essence of the ideal and what is
merely accidental. The military genius does not, when
things go wrong in the field, cling to his tactics at the
expense of his men. The wise portrait painter does not,
when he fails to get a likeness, leave the picture as it is
and attempt an alteration of the sitter. The good cook
does not, when his dishes are found to disagree with the
household, repeat his recipes, demanding in the diners
a greater discernment and better digestions. So with the
reformer, the educationalist, politician, the saint. The
saint is safe enough because he knows, on the authority
of Christ, that the Sabbath was made for man and not
man for the sabbath. But there are only too many reformers who strive after a restored fervour, not because
it would be fervent but because it would be a restoration.
There are only too many educationalists who praise their
educational system, not because it is educational but
because it is a system. There are only too many poli-
ticians who are calling for a cleaner press, not because
they care about purity but because they care very much
about their press.[1] The saint on the other hand has no
such axe to grind: he wants people to be holy because he
has glimpsed something of the holiness of God. And he is
prepared to manipulate the means—as written down, so
to speak, in the hand-book—accordingly. Even the
prophets, though they thundered and blasted at their
flocks, saw always the necessity of 'tempering the breeze

[1] '. . . we must show that an acceptance of the revelation of God as
to the meaning of life has a bearing not only upon holy living, but even
upon sane living; that only those who believe in such a revelation can shape
their own lives correctly and help their fellow-men. Those who do not
accept the revelation, even if they have the best will in the world (which
not all men have), can neither direct their own lives aright nor help other
men—save accidentally and within a very narrow field. From such men
the world has little to hope and an immense amount to fear. And into their
hands the world is tending more and more to fall.' F. J. Sheed, *A Map of
Life*, p. 12.

to the shorn lamb.' They knew that in the eyes of God the lamb came first. It is true that God sometimes shears the lamb very close, but this is only because He does something else at the same time—He saves it. That is why one of His favourite titles is the Good Shepherd. Which is not at all the same thing as the Methodical Shepherd, or the Efficient Shepherd, or the Theoretical Shepherd.

Ezechiel was, as was Our Lord after him, a pastor. That is to say he went out of his way—*his* way—to save souls. The only way to save souls is to use God's way. If, on being tested, the way which is being used is found to be man's way and not God's, then there is only one thing to be done with it and that is to leave it. And the test of such a test must lie in its effect upon man and not in man's effect upon it.

II

Though the ensuing passages are undated it will be seen that the historical references are such that there was no need further to weigh down the material with chronological detail. The chapter is all about Sedecias's secret repudiation of the Chaldean pact and the overtures which he was making towards Egypt. The defection was discovered and dealt with, as we have seen, in 587 B.C. The riddle of the great eagle, which we are about to consider, was therefore proposed some time after Secedias had begun his intrigues and some time before these intrigues were put an end to: in the seventh or eighth year, then, of Sedecias—round about 590-589. The poetic fancy revealed in this section of the Prophecy requires no comment; though sad—as we have already prepared ourselves to expect Ezechiel's images to be—the parable is entirely delicious.

'Son of man, put forth a riddle and speak a parable to the house of Israel, and say: Thus saith the Lord God: A large eagle with great wings, long-limbed, full of feathers and of variety, came to Libanus and

took away the marrow of the cedar. He cropt off
the top of the twigs thereof and carried it away to the
land of Chanaan, and he set it in a city of merchants.
And he took of the seed of the land, and put it in
the ground for seed that it might take root firmly
over many waters; he planted it on the surface of
the earth. And it sprung up and grew into a spread-
ing vine of low stature, and the branches thereof
looked towards him and the roots thereof were under
him. So it became a vine and grew into branches
and shot forth sprigs.'

As this is the first part of the story we can stop for a
moment and make one or two observations. To begin
with this sort of thing is called a 'riddle' in Biblical
language; which does not mean that it was what we would
call a conundrum. The riddle proposed by Ezechiel was
meant to be worked out; it was an allegory in question
form. The story-telling technique is a favourite one with
the preacher in the east; it has the dual merit of demanding some sort of response from the audience and at the
same time allowing to the orator the luxury of elaborate
explanation. The more direct minds of a less leisured
civilisation—our own—are impatient of symbolism and
fable: a pity. With regard to the fable in question,
however, one is inclined to wonder whether it is not
perhaps *too* elaborate for the spoken word—even when
the audience is oriental to its finger tips. I would suggest
that this part of the Prophecy came out in serial form,
and that the people of Tel-Abib were given time to
absorb the details before the 'key' was finally issued
which should make the matter clear. Almost every public
prefers to work out its puzzles (when they are as complicated as this one is) in an arm-chair rather than in a
church, and we feel that Ezechiel had this in mind when he
composed his seventeenth chapter. A further reason for
believing that this prophecy was—if any of them were—
written and not spoken would lie in the fact that it cor

cerns the Jerusalem Jews very closely and the Tel-Abib
Jews hardly at all. But here we are in the world of sheer
conjecture. To return to the second half of the 'riddle,'
and then to provide the explanation:

> 'And there was another large eagle with great
> wings and many feathers. And behold, this vine
> bending as it were her roots towards him stretched
> forth her branches towards him that he might water
> it by the furrows of her plantation. It was planted in
> a good ground upon many waters that it might
> bring forth branches and bear fruit, that it might
> become a large vine. . . . Thus saith the Lord God:
> Shall it prosper then? Shall He not pull up the roots
> thereof and strip off its fruits, and dry up all the
> branches it hath shot forth, and make it wither?'

What a perfectly balanced parable! Even if we had
nothing to tell us what it all referred to we should still
have to admire the artistry of the tale. All the care
which previously went to recording dates seems to go
now to the constructing of proverbs. When speaking
or acting God's message Ezechiel is reasonably direct,
when instructed to compose a pamphlet he allows a
more generous measure of imagery.

> 'The word of the Lord came to me, saying: Say
> to this provoking house: Know you not what these
> things mean?'

The text seems to suggest, as hinted above, that the
explanation took the form of a separate revelation.
Perhaps the less intuitive among Ezechiel's public were
getting the parable wrong. Perhaps the prophet wanted
to make sure that Jerusalem would have no excuse for
ignoring its import. At all events the Lord insisted upon
a commentary to the parable, and it was to be a commentary, moreover, which itself should be couched in
the language of allegory. If the Jews could not be per-
suaded to pray, at least they must be made to *think*.

As soon as the Lord has explained the references He returns to the style of the original fable:

'I Myself will take of the marrow of the high cedar,' He says through the mouth of Ezechiel, 'I will crop off a tender twig from the top of the branches thereof, and I will plant it on a mountain high and eminent. On the mountains of Israel will I plant it, and it shall shoot forth into branches and shall bring forth fruit, and it shall become a great cedar, and all the birds shall dwell under it and every fowl shall make its nest under the shadow of the branches thereof. And all the trees of the country shall know that I the Lord have brought down the high tree and exalted the low tree, and have caused the dry tree to flourish. I the Lord have spoken and have done it.'

Shall we not hear something like this again? Did Our Lady, I wonder, think of that last verse when she spoke the first Magnificat? 'I have brought down the high tree and exalted the low' . . . 'He hath put down the mighty from their place and the humble hath He exalted.' There is very little difference. 'I have caused the dry tree to flourish' . . . 'He hath filled the hungry with good things.' There is very little difference. About the whole of this passage from Ezechiel, indeed, there is a familiar ring: 'all the birds shall dwell under it'—the great cedar— 'and every fowl shall make its nest under the shadow of its branches': these are almost Our Lord's words in picturing His Church. But really we need hardly be surprised at these likenesses: the Author is the same, and He is pointing to the same event—the coming of the Kingdom of Grace.

III

The proximate interpretation of the eagle parable is simply this: Nabuchodonosor is the first eagle.[1] The

[1] The many colours of this eagle's wing are intended to typify the many nations ruled over by Nabuchodonosor.

Jewish race is the cedar in Lebanon. Joachin and Juda's princes are the topmost branches. Babylon is the 'city of merchants.' The stunted vine is again Juda—reduced now on account of the deportations it had suffered. The second eagle is Egypt (great and beautiful also, but lacking the majesty of the other).

Briefly we can see how all this worked out in actual fact. Nabuchodonosor *did* of course crop off the topmost twigs of David's family tree, and set them in his city which was full of merchants. But the eagle had no wish to destroy the country's vegetation altogether; in fact, it 'took the seed of the land' and planted it where it normally belonged; that is to say, Nabuchodonosor took Sedecias and put him on Juda's throne. A 'vine of low stature' was the result. This was inevitable and expected, but what was not inevitable and certainly not to be expected was that the branches should grow in one direction and the roots should grow in another.[1] This was monstrous. All that appeared outwardly was towards Nabuchodonosor, all that was beneath the surface stretched out towards Egypt. 'It was planted in a good ground,' but it used that ground to develop a treacherous growth. 'Shall it prosper then?' asks the Lord, 'Shall it not be dried up? Shall it not wither in the furrows where it grew?'

IV

So much for the direct application of the parable. Indirectly the parable attacks in general all infidelity, all ingratitude, all going after the seductive second string. It is the Bible's reproach to the dread vice of fickleness. This picture from Ezechiel makes a companion to that of the unfruitful vineyard in Isaias. 'What is there that I ought to do more to My vineyard? Was it that I looked that it should bring forth grapes and it hath brought forth wild grapes?'[2] Though the colours are laid on with

---

[1] Sedecias, while openly submitting to Nabuchodonosor, was secretly plotting against him.   [2] Isaias v, 4.

a deeper sadness in Isaias's picture, there is in Ezechiel's the added foreground detail which points to a similar wretchedness in the painter: both men are horrified by the same thing. Not only do they see the Beloved forsaken but they see another lover being chosen in His place.

And then may we not look for still another application to the parable? This time an application which is purely personal and has to do with one man only—Ezechiel.

What follows is going to be sheer guesswork, and since the thread of the story will not be broken if the rest of this section be left out I counsel anyone who is not particularly interested in Ezechiel's inner life to go straight on to the next. I feel merely that if ever a long shot into the hidden depths of a major prophet's soul is permissible it is so here—in a book which has but the airiest claims to Biblical commentary. So long as due warning is given of the conjectural character of the thesis (and of the boresome way in which it will probably be treated) I feel that no conceivable harm can come.

We have suggested (at some length) that Ezechiel was at this period enduring a spiritual 'night.' His ordinary activities were temporarily suspended and he was rather in mid-air. Now, in this state the soul is seldom left unmolested for very long—it might either get bored and give up trying, or else get smug and again give up trying— and therefore some sort of temptation is to be expected. To borrow a metaphor from contemporary civilisation one might say that a spiritual black-out is not merely a matter of sitting in a cellar until the lights are switched on again at the main. The darkness of the spirit, indeed, is not always recognised *as* darkness, and even if it were recognised as such the soul would not be left waiting with folded hands for God to make the next move. Besides being a time of forced inactivity and seeming ineptitude, the time of darkness is one when the vigour of the soul is kept up by some very subtle striving against some very subtle temptations. Thus if we allow that Ezechiel *was* as a fact enduring some such night as we are considering here, then I submit that the particular temptation which assailed him in his darkness was the temptation to make a light of his own.

Put it this way: Ezechiel was disappointed in Tel-Abib, was apprehensive about Jerusalem, was conscious of his ill success, was eager to spread God's word. Is it not possible that suggestions were made to him that he should join his fellow prophet, Daniel, in Babylon? The smaller, and perhaps more devout, Jewish colony may even have invited him. In any case he would have been constantly in touch with the great city, and news would have reached him of conversions, of miracles, of contests between the true religion and the false. Things seemed to be going so much better in Babylon among the heathen than in Tel-Abib among the Jews. With Daniel's influence at court he, Ezechiel, would get a hearing at once; with Daniel's influence, again, it would be easy enough to get himself transferred from Tel-Abib. Perhaps God wanted him in Babylon? Perhaps his talents were being wasted here in Tel-Abib? Perhaps his wife's health would improve in the capital where remedies and distractions and friends were likely to be more plentiful than here in this unsympathetic and uncivilised desert of a place, Tel-Abib? Besides, in Babylon he would be able to lay bare his soul to one who was a master of the spiritual life and whose example would blow into a flame again the fervour which seemed lately to be dying down. Yes, clearly, he could do far more for God with Daniel at his elbow . . . what was the use of stopping on in Tel-Abib?

If all this was going on in Ezechiel's mind then the new significance of the eagle story is fairly obvious. Ezechiel was required to learn from the lesson which he was preaching to others a truth which he was to apply to himself: God, mightier than all other powers, had swooped down into his life like an eagle out of the blue; He had removed him, together with his fellow exiles, from his

native place.   Singled out from among those exiles he,
Ezechiel, had been given a special work to do.   Then,
when the work was felt to have been delayed, stunted, not
quite satisfactory, had come the second eagle . . . and here
was the vine toying with the idea of a new allegiance,
wondering whether after all it might not spread more
swiftly in a slightly different direction.

Is Ezechiel the only one to suffer the same assault upon
his loyalty?   Are not countless light-starved souls, des-
pairing of the dawn, tempted every day and all day to take
it into their own hands to relieve themselves of the full
burden of their night?

> 'Amen I say to you, unless the grain of wheat die,
> itself remaineth alone; but if it die it bringeth forth
> much fruit . . . now is My soul troubled and what
> shall I say? Father, save Me from this hour. But
> for this cause came I unto this hour.'[1]

v

Chapter nineteen of the Prophecy finds Ezechiel still in
the mood for parables. A lamentation is here hurled at the
princes of Israel, and this time the application is so patent
that no explanation is provided. This time also there
seems to be no doubt that the attack was written and not
spoken. For one thing the passage is composed in the
elegiac measure, and it is therefore wildly improbable
that the prophet should have learnt off a metric discourse
by heart and then delivered it to the people of Tel-Abib
in verse form;[2] also, as on the previous occasion of his
preaching a parable, the present sermon relates chiefly
to Jerusalem. The present elegy, which is to do with lions

---

[1] John xii, 24, 25, 27.

[2] The verses are divided by the caesura into unequal lengths, the second
of which (the shorter) drops into the mournful cadence which is the
characteristic of the *kinah* metre. It is a popular device in the dirge poetry
of the east; Ezechiel returns to it in later chapters, notably chapters xxvi,
xxviii, xxxii.

and a vine-plant, refers to the careers of Juda's kings. In order to understand the references only the slightest review need be made of contemporary history: a glance back at Chapter II of this book, or even a recalling eye cast down the chronological table at the beginning, will be quite enough.

'Take up a lamentation for the princes of Israel,' said the Lord, and the lamentation amounted to this: A certain lioness brought up one of her whelps to be a lion capable of catching its prey; the lion used this power to catch, and to devour, men. The reputation of this lion spread quickly, and the result was that the 'nations' captured him and brought him (albeit with some difficulty and injury to themselves) in chains to the land of Egypt. The mother lioness is of course Israel. Joachaz is the young whelp, and the 'nations' are presumably Assyria and Egypt. Pharaoh-Nechao was the Egyptian king who took Joachaz prisoner and had him deported to Egypt, where he died. Joachaz was only twenty-three when he came to the throne, and it was not without a struggle that he was finally secured, so the parable may be considered applicable even down to the details. The story goes on:

> 'But she [the lioness] seeing herself weakened and that her hope was lost, took one of her young lions and set him up for a lion. And he went up and down among the lions and he became a lion, and he learned to catch the prey and to devour men. He learned to make widows and to lay waste cities . . . and the nations came against him and they spread their net over him and they put him into a cage and they brought him in chains to the king of Babylon. . . .'

This story is almost a repetition of the last: a young lion, a precocious power, savage cruelty, capture. But this time it is to Babylon that the prisoner is taken. And so the parable must refer to Joachin. Here the picture changes and Ezechiel goes on:

'Thy mother is like a vine in thy blood planted
by the water: her fruit and her branches have grown
out of many waters. She hath strong rods to make
sceptres for them that bear rule, and her stature was
exalted among the branches; and she saw her height
in the multitude of the branches. But she was
plucked up in wrath and cast on the ground, and the
burning wind dried up her fruit . . . and now she is
transplanted into the desert, in a land not passable
and dry . . . this is a lamentation and shall be for a
lamentation.'

This, coming after the lion passages which are not very
exciting, is a splendid piece of writing; it rounds off in
four verses the message contained in the last five chapters.
'I shall have made their land a wilderness and desolate,'
the Lord had warned His hearers at the close of the
prophet's fifteenth chapter, and now He echoes the threat
with a prophecy of the sin which will bring that threat
into operation. 'She saw her height in the multitude of
her branches'—and was proud of it. *That* was what had
been wrong: Israel had enjoyed her privileges selfishly,
she had appropriated the gifts of God. And now she must
be humbled. Time was when Israel had been a fruitful
vine; now she must be torn up and thrown to one side.
Time was when Israel's royal standards had risen higher
than those of other kingdoms; now even the sceptre of
Sedecias must be wrested from his grasp and the standards
of Babylon be substituted for those of the Chosen Race.
Israel must eat out her heart in the desert, 'in a land
not passable and dry.'

CHAPTER X

THE ELDERS COME AGAIN

IN the twentieth chapter of the Prophecy the taciturn elders are represented as calling upon Ezechiel for the third time; the occasion is carefully recorded in the prophet's diary. 'In the seventh year in the fifth month, the tenth day of the month, there came the ancients of Israel to enquire of the Lord, and they sat before me.' So in August of the year 590, four years before the fall of Jerusalem and six years after the prophet's arrival, there was another stir in the affairs of Tel-Abib which needed the attention of him whom God had evidently chosen for the work of guiding Jewish souls. The delegates seem again to have represented the growing uneasiness among the exiles as to their chances of a return to Jerusalem. The colonists also wanted to know what sort of a Jerusalem it would be to which they were—still—expecting to return. There had been much talk about the Holy City's impending doom, but after all the Holy City was still intact. Perhaps Ezechiel would have some further light to throw . . . no one would think any the less of him were he to modify some of his previous statements; and, if the prophet still proved obstinate about Jerusalem's future, one could always write home and find out what was the opinion on the subject in the Holy City itself. In other words, the Tel-Abib Jews wanted to get inside information without having to commit themselves. The Lord's mouthpiece was, on this showing, for the Jewish convenience and not for the Jewish conscience. It was the same story over again and one which called for much the same answer. But this time, instead of sketching the future, Ezechiel reviewed the past. Refusing to be used as a planchette table, the prophet held up the mirror to Jewish history and gave to his enquirers a neat survey of all that had led up to the present situation. Admittedly, and of necessity, this part of the Prophecy is not as thrilling as some of those chapters that have gone before and others which will come after, but it has its place in the prophet's life and so cannot be altogether passed over.

From the beginning (so Ezechiel was instructed to tell the elders) God's dealings with His Chosen People had been characterised by certain fixed principles. His demand for the undivided allegiance of that People had been made easy to bear by reason of the very special preservation which they had enjoyed at His hand. And yet *every time* He had been disappointed. While they were still in Egypt He had asked them to keep away from idols: they had clung to them. In bringing His People out from Egypt all He had wanted of them was faith and renunciation of heathen ways: He had got neither. Throughout the Sinaitic period He had safeguarded their integrity by providing for them a legislation and a liturgy: they had rejected His statutes and profaned His Sabbaths.[1] Generation after generation it had been the same thing. It was only because He *was* the God of the Jews, only to justify His Name before mankind, that again and again He had spared the 'provoking' house of Israel.[2] Were the Jews able, then, to trace God's finger in their history up to date? Yes, indeed, they could hardly do otherwise! Very well, that same God had placed one among them who heralded an approaching doom: it was their business to believe and act accordingly. The past must serve as a guarantee of the future: if God was in one, He was also in the other. And the elders must not enquire any further. No answer would be given to those who insisted upon walking in the evil ways of their fathers. Did they want to know *how* and exactly *when* the punishment would come upon them? He, Jehovah, was not an oracle that He should be questioned so. But they would know soon enough, these elders, that His dominion over Israel was as assured now as it had ever been; and just as He had taken their ancestors from the

[1] 12, 13.   [2] 14, 15.

heathenism of Egypt, so He would take their children from the heathenism of Chaldea. But in His good time, not theirs. And *then* would His name be great before the nations. In the meantime, however:

> 'I will kindle a fire in thee [O Israel], and I will burn in thee every green tree and every dry tree; the flame of the fire shall not be quenched, and every face shall be burned in it, from the south even to the north. And all flesh shall see that I, the Lord, have kindled it and it shall not be quenched. And I [Ezechiel] said: Ah, ah, ah, Lord God, they say of me: Doth not this man speak by parables?'

And so the chapter ends. The concluding verse is interesting because it shows not only that he knew very well what was being said of him but that he still resented what was being said. We might have supposed that by this time Ezechiel was sufficiently holy to have laughed at the criticisms of his public: apparently not—he hated them. Or if he did not hate the ridicule which he attracted at least he was still human enough to give to God as an excuse for his failure the ridicule which he knew that his mission evoked. There seems even to be the suggestion of a reproach in the prophet's words—the reproach which says, 'It isn't *my* fault I preach parables; I'd have gone about it quite differently. It was You, if You remember,' etc. And if the prophets of God can say this sort of thing, there is consolation for us who so often feel it.

CHAPTER XI

THE DEATH OF EZECHIEL'S WIFE

I

TRAGEDY is never very far from Ezechiel. Sometimes the dramatic nature of his self-expression causes us to mistake tragedy for melodrama, but when we look closer we see that the realities of Ezechiel's life are singularly untheatrical. The truth of it is that the prophet's experience differed little from that of most people. The real crises of people's lives—those occasions when the essential self is called into play—are the moments when life is acting strongly upon the man and not when the person in question is doing all the acting. Great renunciations and momentous decisions are merely man's handling of given material. What is far more important is the behaviour of man under the handling of God. It is this which measures the success or failure of life. The moments of real progress are those when the yielding (but apparently unready) soul is swept by God from its self-appointed course and planted in the way of God's choosing. Patient in the hand of the Lord—such was the determining quality of Ezechiel's sanctity.

The incident now to be considered is contained in the twenty-fourth chapter of the text. This means that we are leaving out three chapters of the Prophecy and nearly four years of the period. With the twenty-first chapter (we left off at the end of the twentieth) Ezechiel is seen to be hurling thunderbolts into the thick of Jerusalem's crowds; in the twenty-second we have an enumeration of the sins to which Juda has been more especially addicted; the twenty-third, branching off slightly from the theme, exposes the ingratitude and defection of Samaria. Since the matter dealt with in these chapters is either not very interesting or not very relevant, there seems excuse enough for passing them over in this way.[1] Particularly need we have no scruple in so doing when we see from the chapter headings that much of the ground has either been gone over before or else is to be gone over later. So much for textual sequence. From the chronological point of view, however, the gap left by the removed passages will have to be filled in when we have considered the death of Ezechiel's wife. The reason for this is that there are several prophecies which were delivered before the year 587 but which come in the text after the events attributed to that year. This is the only instance (I think) where Ezechiel takes liberties with the sequence, so in order to make the Prophecy easier to follow as it stands I have ventured to do the same.

Even with regard to the chapter in hand it will not be found necessary to begin at the beginning. All that need be said about the first fifteen verses is that they give another riddle or parable illustrating the collapse of Jerusalem, and that this (the story of the rusted cauldron) is not to be mistaken for one of Ezechiel's acted dumb-shows; it was certainly written or spoken, and not, as verses three to five might lead one to suppose, performed.

The chapter is meticulously dated; in fact this time it is the Lord Himself who insists on the exactitude: 'Son of man, write thee the name of this day.' It is true 'this day' refers to the cauldron revelation and not the death of the prophet's wife, but the two incidents certainly took place in the same year, 587 B.C.

> 'Son of man, behold I take from thee the desire of thy eyes with a stroke. And thou shalt not lament nor weep neither let thy tears run down. Sigh in silence and make no mourning for the dead.'

[1] These chapters are full of references to events of the period; for a study of the allusions see Davidson and Streane's *Ezechiel*, pp. 174-190. This work, in the *Cambridge Bible Series*, is perhaps the best all round exposition of the subject. Not strictly critical or tiresomely historical, it gives a good idea of the man, of the Book, and of the times.

We have not said much about Ezechiel's wife up till
now, and the reason for this is that Ezechiel has not
either. The death, short though the account of it is,
was *the* great landmark in the outward life and inward
development of the prophet. 'The desire of thy eyes'
tells us how devoted he was to his wife; 'let not thy tears
run down' shows what a pain her loss would be to him.
It is a good thing that we should know of Ezechiel's
love. We would otherwise be inclined to sum him up
on his public life alone, and so to consider him as a
rather fierce, and a possibly loveless, fanatic; but that
his married life was a success is a fact which brings a
new warmth into the picture. It seems almost as if his
home life was so dear and intimate to him that he could
bring it into his published work only at the Lord's command and in the briefest terms. He was thirty-three
or thirty-four years old when 'the desire of his eyes'
was taken away from him. The Lord gave His servant
very little warning: the whole thing, as we shall see,
was desperately sudden. But it was not the suddenness
of the death which was to rob Ezechiel of the relief of
tears; it was the command of God, 'thou shalt not weep,'
which prevented even the comfort which man finds in
mourning. And if sigh he must, then Ezechiel must
sigh in secret and in silence. . . . God does not spare His
friends. And not only must all show of sorrow be avoided
but all ordinary show of well-being must be kept up.
'Let the tire of thy head be upon thee, and thy shoes
upon thy feet, and cover not thy face nor eat the meat of
mourners.'[1] Such were the instructions of the Lord.
So that when it came to his own life and not that of
Juda the man of signs must show no sign; and because
there have been so many signs before, the absence of
signs now would be all the more significant.

[1] The 'tire' was probably the white turban which would distinguish
him as a priest. To go barefoot was the traditional sign of mourning.
Sorrow was also expressed by veiling the lower part of the face. The
'meat of mourners' refers to the custom of pressing food upon the bereaved.

'So I spoke to the people in the morning, and my wife died in the evening. And I did in the morning [i.e. the morning following] as He had commanded me.'

The words of this verse throb with the pathos of what is left unsaid. The three verses so far quoted cover a bare thirty-six hours of time: the revelation on the first day, the preaching next morning, the death that evening, and the resumption of normal life with the dawn of the third day. There is no waste of words and no waste of time: the prophet has been faithful to the Lord's demand for a silent mourning. No hint of resentment, no hint of his feelings, no hint—even—of a prayer. The text runs straight on:

'And the people said to me: Why dost thou not tell us what these things mean which thou doest? And I said to them: The word of the Lord came to me saying: Speak to the house of Israel: Thus saith the Lord God: Behold I will profane My sanctuary, the glory of your realm and the thing that your eyes desire . . . your sons and your daughters shall fall by the sword. And you shall do as I have done: you shall not cover your faces nor shall you eat the meat of mourners . . . you shall not weep.'

Notice first that as soon as they had heard of his wife's death the people of Tel-Abib came to express their sympathy. The fact that it was to commiserate and not to question is to be insisted upon because there are those who would try and prove from the text that the whole thing was just another parable and that the people were puzzled at so *macabre* a 'riddle.' No, what happened surely was this: the people heard what had happened and, coming to show sympathy, were surprised to find that instead of being met by a stricken husband they were met by an apparently indifferent one. And it was *this* which made them say, 'tell us what these things mean.'

The people of Tel-Abib were not asking about a fictitious wife's death (which they could have understood) but about a very real husband's unusual behaviour (which they could not).

Ezechiel explained. The beloved city, the desire of your eyes, will shortly perish. You will find yourselves doing as I, in my personal affliction, am doing—you will dispense with formal mourning. But where I have done so because God commanded it, you will do so because you will be too dazed to notice the omission. Grief will stun you, and shame will drive your tears, bitter but unshed, into the caverns of your souls.

II

'Behold I take from thee the desire of thy eyes with a stroke.' Are we to believe that when a man is as holy as Ezechiel was, he does not really feel the loss of somebody he loves? Ezechiel's own case seems to show the opposite. Death is always frightful for those who remain, and except in the highest point of the soul it makes little difference if one is holy or if one is not. And the reason for this is that death's frightfulness is in some sort a thing apart. I mean that to those whose religion means any-thing at all real, the thing about another's death which is hard to bear is not connected with resentment at the sacrifice, or, still less, with doubts as to whether departed souls are or are not better off than we. One may have a firm grasp of the theory and yet find in practice that it is of little help. Death seems to escape all theory. We wonder sometimes how this can be. Is it that our sorrow sweeps us away from God? Does the pain which we suffer argue that the human love was wrong, and unrelated to the love of God? Have we been so little affected by years of trying to do God's will that when a personal grief comes crashing into our lives we have nothing but a few dry generalisations with which to meet it? Has there been self-deception all along, and do we—loving His creatures so much—love Him too little? Surely not. Is it not rather that we are *meant* to feel these things? If there is human imperfection in loneliness and the sense of our loss, perhaps it is that we need to be reminded of our humanity. Perhaps in our pursuit of the supernatural we have begun to discredit, intellectually, the natural. Then death comes to remind us of the natural. We cannot afford to leave out *anything* in our way to God, and sometimes it is necessary that He should convince us of this by some violent upheaval such as the death of one we love. Turning our lives upside down, death comes to teach us the lesson of the Incarnation, and we realise suddenly that what we have left out in our spiritual formation is something human. But we *may* not leave out this human thing. The Word was made flesh, and the key to our problem is in the Sacred Humanity. By the death of another we learn more of Christ: by the life of Christ we learn more of the meaning of another's death.

It is always our tendency to drive a wedge between God's spiritual and God's natural order, and so it is that we see the human love in our souls measured against the love we have for God. And we are frightened accordingly. But true love is a coat without seam, and it is we who make of it a thing of parts. If only we loved God rightly and all that was His, we should not feel so lost when all natural consolation is suddenly withdrawn; it is only because the two do not flow into each other that the loss of one renders the other comfortless. Death should leave us sad, yes, but not at sea in our misery.

And even when we have said all this we see that here is again a theory, again an attempt to fortify ourselves against our grief with abstract consolations.

Leaving theory aside then, and looking at it from another angle, what is it that hurts us when we see our friends die? For most of us it is the shock of seeing the relentless finality to what we knew as life. In a way we could never have foreseen or provided against, we realise

how utterly cut off we are from the *personality* of the one
we knew. It is not that we feel cut off from the bigger
spiritual relationships which can go on existing between
one human soul and another—as accepted in the doctrine
of the Communion of Saints—but cut off rather from those
hundred and one lesser points of contact which go to
make up life: those countless secondary things which
had meant so much (when looked back upon) but which
seemed (when enjoyed in the ordinary run of life) of
such momentary value. We become suddenly aware—
we'd have known all along if we had thought about
it, but now we *know*—that we can never get in touch
again with, for instance, the other's sense of humour,
with the other's appreciations of the things which we
appreciate, with the other's prejudices and points of
view. We become suddenly aware that for the rest of
our lives we shall miss the familiar gestures, mannerisms,
shynesses, ways of pronouncing things, and so on. The
voice is silent—yes, we had expected it would be—but
that the yawns and sudden bursts of laughter will never
be repeated, *this* is the part that shocks us to the heart.
In such a sense all deaths are sudden deaths.

Why, we ask, does death affect us like this? It can
only mean (so we argue against ourselves) that we are
being horribly selfish: we hate having to give up *all*, and
though we are prepared to sacrifice the important things
we find it hard to yield on the little ones; and this shrinking
from sacrifice (so we go on in our self-analysis) obscures
the truth which reason accepts—namely, that these
secondary things don't matter because the really
important ones do. But is this quite fair? Surely there is
a less condemning explanation. If we let our memories
take us back to those occasions we have mentioned—
those moments which were taken for granted when all
was well but which seem charged with meaning now—
what do they spell for us but exquisite happiness in
retrospect? We look upon them as passing moments of

true joy. *Passing* moments. But surely the truth of it is that they were not passing moments. They gave true joy because they had something in them of eternity. They stand out in our memories because they were so true that not even time could falsify them. To have enjoyed in this way is not to have enjoyed selfishly, it is to have enjoyed rightly. It means that our enjoyment has come from others and has come from God. Which is where our enjoyment ought to come from. It is right that we should be happy in another's happiness. And it is precisely because God is Love that love's moments, however insignificant they seem, are everlasting.

Memories may become blurred, wounds may be healed, affections may be extended to wider circles, but those recollections which stab us when another dies are not there because they are momentary, they are there because they are eternal. Human love, since it is in part divine, is not mortal merely; love is essentially immortal, but since it is enjoyed by human beings it can be realised only intermittently. In moments. It is the momentary character of our experience which makes us judge our love, in retrospect, to have been selfish: it is its immortality which should convince us that, in origin and end at all events, it is divine.

And so we get back to where we were before—that the love of God and the love of His creatures are one thing. If chasm there was between the loyalties, Christ has bridged it in His Sacred Person.

III

Added to the sufferings which we have been considering there is—still bound up with another's death—a further pain of which Ezechiel was almost certainly the victim at this time. It is the pain which those must bear who have had entrusted to them by God the care of a particularly favoured soul. Ezechiel had guided his wife in the ways of the spirit; he had been—as he had been to the people

of Tel-Abib but in a far more living sense where his wife
was concerned—a channel of grace from God. And now
this soul was removed from his influence : he could no
longer be of use. The giving of those things that mattered
most in life had formed a new relationship: he had given
and he had taken, and the bond had always been God.
From now onwards (he tells himself as he looks on the
face of his dead wife) this sacred intercourse can be only
indirect. Yes, but how mistaken to worry about that!
Let us hope that Ezechiel's grief did not blind him to a
better view. On earth (he could have told himself) *we*
give, and have no more to give: in heaven God gives,
and gives infinitely . . . let us not wish our friends back
in a world where we might go on giving, but where the
infinite giving of God should be delayed.

But of all this Ezechiel says nothing. Earlier on in this
book I have observed that the prophet, though a theatrical
person in some ways, was not in the least melodramatic
when it came to the real crises of his life. The three
verses which give the story of his wife's death bear this
out. Those writers who, denying the reality of the death,
suggest that the story was invented for literary affect, are
guilty (so it seems to me) of impertinence and even of
irreverence. That a prophet of God should use as a make-
weight to his book something so sacred as the death of
his wife is unthinkable.

IV

The siege of Jerusalem and the death of Ezechiel's wife
have more than a symbolical connexion: the two events
are linked together in point of time. Ezechiel knew on
the night of his wife's illness that the long threatened
conflict was upon his people. He had preached about it
only that morning; he had acted it for years; he
had prayed and thought about it since the Lord had
called him to His service. And now had come his personal
sorrow driving it out of his mind. It is a curious and

perhaps humiliating fact that the human organism cannot cope with more than one very violent emotion at the same time; the greater anxiety completely obliterates the less. Jerusalem was forgotten. In a day or two Ezechiel would have to be preaching about it again,[1] but for today there cou'd be one sole preoccupation. And as a matter of fact for the rest of his life the death would be infinitely more real to him than the city's fall; he seems, as we shall see on a later page, to have ceased worrying about Jerusalem, once it had been destroyed. To the Jews the mention of Ezechiel's loss would for years to come remind them of the great catastrophe; to the prophet it would be the other way about—he would date the fall by his wife's death. God sees to it that there is nothing nearer to a man than his own cross.

Then, when it was all over and the dawn had seen the end of Ezechiel's agonised vigil, there would have been the fresh agony of having to pick up again the threads of daily life. Everything to be resumed where, two nights ago, it had been interrupted. To comment upon this phase of the prophet's way to God would be to intrude beyond the bounds which may reasonably be allowed to commentators. This much we can say, however, that when Ezechiel looked out over the rooftops of Tel-Abib on the morning following his wife's death he knew beyond possibility of contradiction that though he would go on for God's sake doing the same things as before, he would go on doing them in a very different way. In the grey dawn of a day which in all respects save one was like many days before and after, Ezechiel (aged thirty-three or four) felt suddenly old. The desire of his eyes had gone from him.

[1] xxiv, 18-21.

CHAPTER XII

AFTERWARDS

'In that day when he that escapeth shall come to
thee to tell thee, in that day, I say, shall thy mouth
be opened . . . and thou shalt speak and thou shalt
be silent no more; and thou shalt be unto them for a
sign.'

This is the sequel to what has just gone before. 'He
that escapeth' refers to the messenger of Jerusalem's fall.
As soon as the news reaches you (is the Lord's promise to
Ezechiel) you will be freed for good from these periods
of dumbness which have so far attended your prophetical
career; you will, moreover, be listened to. The Jewish
people will see at last that you have been 'unto them
for a sign.' I don't say you will be a success and find
favour, but I do say that the vindication of your prophecies will be recognised.

Early in the year 586, then, Tel-Abib would have
learned of the sack of the Holy City. The news announced,
the exiles went about their duties listlessly, silently, hopelessly—as Ezechiel had said they would. No possibility
of a return now . . . nothing to return to. Dazed by the
thought of their own stupidity as much as by the thought
of what their fellow Jews had suffered at home, the settlers
in Chaldea had not even the energy to cry out or rebel.
Ezechiel, woe to the man, had been right all along.

Ezechiel had now been a widower for some months.
He may have been a solitary figure but he was probably
not a lonely one. God compensates eventually, even in
this life, when He takes away love for the sake of Love.
Perhaps by this time the desire of the eyes was already
being replaced by the desires of the soul. But whether
or not his loss had been made good interiorly we know
that loneliness was not outwardly the prophet's lot:
people came to see him and ask him questions, and, if

we may read between the lines, the answers he gave them were less bitter than the kind of thing he had given them hitherto. True, there was nothing very much to be bitter about, but in any case Ezechiel had now no quarrel with mankind. The man was mellowing—at thirty-four! And the Jews must have noticed it. We can imagine them attributing all the wrong causes to the change. So it was as a bachelor recluse (they would have concluded) that Ezechiel was at last coming into his element; so he could now afford to be more affable— having had his predictions verified; so without that little wife of his to keep him in a constant state of anxiety he could at last enjoy, etc. . . . In some such way as this would the people of Tel-Abib have expressed their belief that Ezechiel had come through his difficult years with flying, though suitably restrained, colours. And up to a point they were, one feels, right. Unless, that is, the speculations put forward in this book have been hopelessly wide of the mark we *can* be confident of a dawn: Ezechiel *does* seem to have got over the worst part of his night. Does this sound unlikely—that the prophet's dawn should follow his wife's death? Not altogether, when we find that the Day of Resurrection was not far separated from the Night of Crucifixion.

In Ezechiel—if we care to regard it so—the story of Sedecias and the song of St. John of the Cross were being rehearsed. We have made the latter application to the soul in general, it can now be made to the soul of Ezechiel in particular.

> *Forth unobserved I went,*
> *My house being now at rest.*

CHAPTER XIII

HISTORICAL INTERLUDE

I

THE group of prophecies now to be considered is composed of the seven chapters referring to the 'nations round about.' These prophecies were published, as suggested on an earlier page, before the destruction of Jerusalem. At least this is the view which will be followed in the present study; certain writers assign the chapters in question to a later date and give good reasons for their opinion,[1] but, weighing up the arguments and laying no claim to infallibility, I presume to side with those who see in this group a written corpus of prophecy composed at a time when the prophet was unable to speak. It is interesting to note that in Isaias and Jeremias there are corresponding groups of prophecies foretelling evil to much the same list of peoples. Ezechiel deals with such familiar names among Israel's traditional enemies as Ammon, Sidon, Moab, Edom, Philistia, Tyre—an enormous amount of space is devoted to Tyre—and Egypt. We will confine ourselves to Ezechiel's treatment of Egypt. Before, however, examining what the prophet has to say about this nation it is as well to note that he seems to have nothing to say about another nation—and a more immediately menacing one—Babylonia. Babylonia was to collapse like the rest, and one would have thought that it might find a place among the condemned. Was it that Ezechiel feared a reprisal if he published indictments

[1] Once his mind is relieved of the burden which he has had to deliver to Juda, Ezechiel is able (so it is held by some critics) to devote his attention to wider fields. Since, moreover, the prophet's main theme from the time of the destruction onwards is to be the Restoration of the race, it is fitting that he should preface his scheme of reconstruction with a series of Judgements passed on other nations: the removal of menace from abroad was a necessary step towards peace at home. The prophecies in question are contained in chapters xxv-xxxii.

against his captors? Hardly. A much more likely reason for his silence would be that he had ceased to regard his captors *as* captors. We have already seen how easy was the yoke which was pressed upon the Hebrew exiles, and if his was anything like the attitude of Daniel towards Chaldean authority we can judge that Ezechiel would not have resented Nabuchodonosor's rule in the least; indeed he would have regarded it as being in some sort a blessing—a God-given, and by no means a severe, instrument of correction. Certainly this reticence of the prophet's about Babylon is a good reason for believing that this section of prophecy was written before the fall of Jerusalem, because had Babylon, at the time of his writing, already reduced the Holy City to ashes, it is unlikely that Ezechiel would have omitted all mention of the similar fate in store for the Chaldean capital.

II

When we read all that Ezechiel had to say about Egypt we are inclined to wonder why he went into the matter so fully. The reason for this emphasis on the southern kingdom is partly because Egypt's history, more than any other's on the prophet's list, was bound up with that of Israel; partly also it is because Ezechiel wanted above all things to avoid, when the time should come for the Jewish nation to reassemble itself, any sort of reliance being put upon Egypt. The Chosen People must grow up Pharaoh-shy.

These prophecies which are directed against Egypt are characterised by the liveliest imagery, and are well worth reading; here we can satisfy ourselves with a summary. (It must be admitted that if there is one slight drawback to the prophet Ezechiel it is that he is inclined to be diffuse.) The first prophecy—all about a crocodile who boasts that the Nile is of his own making—threatens Egypt for its pride and general self-sufficiency. God tells the crocodile that he will be hooked by the jaws and

dragged to the dry land, and that the fishes which have
been clinging to his scales will so attract birds and beasts
of prey that the crocodile's body will soon be consumed.
Because Egypt has boasted, and has been unfaithful to
her promises to Israel, she will be drawn away (this is
the explanation) from her native river-bed.   Nabuchodonosor will come and scatter her resources; for forty
years Egypt will be a prostrate power; and when this time
is over she will gather strength again, but only such
strength as will enable her to rank among the lesser
nations.   Never again will Egypt be a temptation to
Israel—she will have proved herself a broken reed.
With this in store for Egypt, the Lord turns now to
Nabuchodonosor and assures him that, in recognition
of his services rendered to God's cause in the matter of
Babylon's campaign against Tyre, the Egyptian empire
will be delivered into his hands.[1]

Jeremias[2] has much the same complaint to make
against Egypt, and foretells much the same future. The
trouble is that we do not know for certain how far the
predictions of the two prophets were verified as regards
Egypt.   The cuneiform accounts of Nabuchodonosor's
invasion of Egypt are, perhaps purposely, vague.   We
know that he embarked upon a campaign in 568 B.C. to
subdue the rival power, but information is not forth-
coming as to the result. He may have made an earlier

[1] Nabuchodonosor spent thirteen years (585-572 B.C.) in reducing Tyre,
the capital of Phœnicia. This was the hardest won triumph of his long
reign, and even then the fruits of victory were so inconsiderable that the
Jewish historian Josephus is unwilling to record a decision either way.
But even if Tyre was not actually sacked, certain it is that a Babylonian
official took up his headquarters there and acted as a sort of prefect. If we
had only the single reference in Ezechiel to go upon we would have reason
to believe that Nabuchodonosor was strictly successful in his campaign,
but as a fact we have other information—also from Ezechiel—which suggests
that this was not the case. The second reference (xxviii, xxix) is from a
passage dated 570 B.C. and so was written two years after the siege was
over. The earlier reference is, since it is a prediction and not a statement
of past history, another indication in favour of the view that these chapters
we are dealing with were written before Jerusalem's fall.   [2] xliii.

expedition as well; but, though this suits the Ezechiel programme better from the point of view of time it leaves unanswered the question as to why, if it was as successful as Ezechiel said it would be, he had to make another a few years later. The manner of Egypt's decline and the date of it we simply do not know; but what we do know is that Egypt did decline very rapidly, and that for about forty years it suffered a complete eclipse. It is also certain that when Egypt next appeared in the political arena it was, on account of the widespread Persian domination, of no great political standing.

It might here be asked why Persia—if under Cambyses and his successors it was to make so much difference to the civilisation of that part of the world in future years— is not mentioned in the list of nations enumerated by Ezechiel. I can only suggest that the prophet's mission at this time was not to mention all the nations which should rise and fall in years to come but to mention particularly those which might stand in the way of Juda's promised destiny. Ezechiel's present business was to call down woes on enemy peoples, not to read the fortunes of friendly ones. It must also be remembered that there was no particular need for Ezechiel to say anything about a race which had already been heralded with great fulness by Isaias.

III

In order to follow Ezechiel's highly characteristic thirty-first chapter we shall need to survey some more non-Judean history. The text gives us another cedar tree; the critics give us innumerable branches. This time the cedar represents Egypt and not, as previously, Juda. The prophecy amplifies what has already been said about the southern nation, and adds a few pretty details of its own; it is a grim little pen-picture. The Pharaoh whom it mentions is most probably Hophra (or Apries as he is sometimes called), the man upon the throne at the time of Jerusalem's fall. It was he, who according to Herodotus the Greek historian of the fifth century B.C., stirred up Phœnicia into a state of rebellion against Nabuchodonosor.[1]

> 'The word of the Lord came to me saying: Son of man, speak to Pharaoh king of Egypt and to his people: To whom art thou like in thy greatness? Behold, the Assyrian was like a cedar in Libanus, with fair branches and full of leaves, of high stature and his top was elevated among the thick boughs. The waters nourished him and the deep set him on high, the streams thereof ran round about his roots, and it sent forth its rivulets into all the trees of the country. Therefore was his height exalted above all the trees of the country.'

It will be noticed that the text (taken from the Vulgate) says that the 'Assyrian' was like a cedar. We would expect of course that the cedar would be compared to the Egyptian and not the Assyrian. The prophecy was addressed to Pharaoh, so why bring in a nation which had ceased to exist generations ago, and whose history and culture bore little relation in any case to the history and culture of Egypt? Dr. Davidson has no scruple in saying 'It is evident that the Assyrian has nothing to do here,' and he points out that where the same verse is repeated later on Egypt is mentioned and not Assyria.[2] Dr. Barnes, writing in *The New Commentary on Holy Scripture*, is as emphatic. H. A. Redpath is less positive but clearly supports this view; his is the theory that by the addition of one Hebrew letter we can have, instead of 'the Assyrian,' the name of a certain box-wood tree which is a kind of cedar, which certainly grows in Lebanon, which might quite easily have been copied down wrong by a careless

---

[1] This was the rebellion which elicited Nabuchodonosor's campaign against Tyre.

[2] *Op. cit.* p. 244. Dr. Lofthouse, in an article in *The Story of The Bible*, takes it for granted that Ezechiel is referring to Egypt.

scribe. Which is quite probably correct. It must be admitted, however, that Fr. Hugh Pope accepts the text as we have quoted it, and so makes the whole prophecy refer to the past and not to the future. Thus, with Fr. Pope's weighty judgement in mind, it is not without considerable misgivings that I have chosen to follow the less strict reading of Ezechiel's words. [1]

The parable goes on to tell of the fowls which came to lodge in the cedar's branches and the beasts which gave birth to their young in its shadow. It became the envy of Libanus as the tree of Pride had become the envy of Eden. The cedar gloried in its magnificence, and from its great height it looked down upon the other trees in Libanus. Had it looked *up*—seems to be the implication— all would have been well, but it chose to measure its stature by the 'fir-trees and the plane-trees' which it had outgrown. And from this it was not a great step for the cedar to demand the homage of the rest. What a perfect meditation on the virtue of humility! As long as we keep our eyes on what is above us we are in no serious danger of falling: as soon as we look down we get giddy and lose our foothold. The reason why Lucifer fell was because he considered the distance between himself and the lesser angels instead of considering the distance which existed between himself and God. Lucifer looked down and found he had no head for heights. No such dizziness was Mary's when, from an even greater height, she kept her eyes on God and told the world that it was He who had placed her where she was. The same with Paul, the same with Teresa, the

[1] It is possible that Fr. Pope has not met the ingenious theory of the box-wood and the root-origin of the word 'Assyria.' In a retreat discourse delivered at Worth Priory some years ago Fr. Pope spoke at some length on this 'cedar of Libanus,' and certainly there was no doubt in his mind then: he never mentioned the other view, and I for one am very glad he did not—the discourse could be enjoyed without distraction. (The particular discourse, incidentally, was not about the virtue of humility as one might expect, but upon religious unity.

same with all the saints. If we start measuring our own shadow we have to look down to see where it is.

But to return to Ezechiel's cedar. As a punishment for its self-esteem it was felled to the ground, and the impact of its fall was so great that it disturbed the surrounding country. 'All the trees of the field trembled and I shook the nations with the sound of his fall,' says the Lord. The man chosen to cut down the cedar was of course Nabuchodonosor, and it is one of those ironies which occasionally appear in the pages of Scripture that he, Nabuchodonosor, was to suffer much the same treatment as that which he was now meting out to Egypt. A great tree came into Nabuchodonosor's life; it was cut down but its stump remained.[1] So with the tree which was Egypt: it was levelled to the ground but its roots continued to live. Many generations later Egypt became—as every school-boy knows—the 'granary of Rome.' But there is all the difference in the world between being a granary and being able—as metaphorically Egypt had once been able—to make a corner in grain.

IV

The chapter which follows in the text is only an enlargement in different form upon the foregoing theme. It is a highly complicated dirge over fallen Egypt; so complicated is it, indeed, that to go into all its textual possibilities and political applications would be infinitely tedious. True there is a pleasant smattering of dragons, lions, fishes and inundating rivers, but there is no sort of plot about the whole, and the parable-motif is so thinly spread that we can confine ourselves merely to saying that the Egyptian king referred to is again Pharaoh Hophra, that the overflowing river is the Nile, and that the animals are the Babylonian hordes. The chapter is really two prophecies, not one: the second, which is even more involved than the first, being delivered a

[1] Daniel iv.

fortnight after the other. In this last half of the chapter the 'lament' over Egypt gives place to an account of the companions which will accompany Egypt into the pit of Sheol. Assyria (which had come to an end as a nation at the close of the seventh century B.C.) will be there; Elam also (whose destruction was prophesied by Jeremias during Sedecias's reign); Nosoch and Thubal 'and all their multitude' are on the list; the oft-condemned Edom (whose judgement Ezechiel had foretold three years previously); and lastly all the 'princes of the north and the hunters'—particularly (though our text does not mention them by name) the Sidonians. This vast army of the reprobate will be seen by Pharaoh of Egypt, and, so debased will his sense then be, he will take comfort in the thought that he is not alone in his evils. 'He was comforted concerning the multitude which was slain by the sword.' This is a depressing and, one must admit it, a not very interesting chapter of the Prophecy.

CHAPTER XIV

EZECHIEL'S MISSION RESTATED

I

THE next seven chapters of the prophecy form a separate block in the Book, and breathe a somewhat different spirit from what has gone before. This latter fact bears out the change in Ezechiel's general temper which we have been watching. The first chapter of this section is transitional—linking up with the foregoing—and deals with a twofold responsibility: one on the part of the prophet *as* a prophet, the other on the part of the people as regards each one's individual obligation towards the Lord. The remaining six chapters[1] of the group treat of Israel's restoration and the reign of peace. Taking here the first chapter only, we can leave until a later page Ezechiel's ideas on the ideal ruler and the ideal ruled.

This thirty-third chapter must have been written not later than two years after the fall of Jerusalem; in the twenty-first verse we read that the fugitives from Juda were just beginning to arrive in Tel-Abib, and this did not take place until some eighteen months after the Holy City's evacuation. The general drift of this passage is to the effect that, with the passing of the old order of things and the introduction of a new, a fuller consciousness must be developed in the Jewish mind of God's purpose not only with the whole race but with every member of it. Under the new dispensation it is the moral aspect of things which alone will count for anything.

Just as the prophet's original mission was initiated by a close packed instruction as to what his particular function was to be, so now—when the new phase of Ezechiel's ministry is about to begin—there is a revelation from the Lord which reasserts the position. Again it is as a

[1] xxxiv-xxxix.

'watchman' that the prophet is to respond to his vocation: if he fails to sound the alarm, no one else will do it for him. It is a fearful responsibility:

> 'If the watchman see the sword coming and sound not the trumpet . . . and the sword come and cut off a soul from among them, he indeed is taken away in his iniquity, but I will require his blood at the hand of the watchman.'

Was there any danger that Ezechiel would *not* sound the alarm when the time came? No, surely the above verse is intended as a preparation for the instruction as to the *manner* in which alarms are to be sounded.

> 'Say to them: As I live, saith the Lord, *I desire not the death of the wicked but that the wicked turn from his way and live* . . . why will you die, O house of Israel?'

How tender is this compared with what has gone before, how much nearer is this to our ideas of God! Only now, when we are half way through Ezechiel's Prophecy, do we find the Lord doing justice to Himself; only now does Ezechiel learn to shed that slight harshness which was his at the start. It is strange to think that a second call is needed before the prophet can know—*really* know—what every Catholic child is taught when it makes its First Confession. It is at least comforting to know that Ezechiel was one of the Old Testament writers who *did* arrive at the doctrine which teaches 'that the benignity of God leadeth unto penance.'[1]

And since we have flowed over into the new dispensation we can look for a moment at the account of another calling—the summons of Don Bosco in A.D. 1824. It will illustrate the manner in which true apostolates are conducted. 'Many were swearing and using foul words. In order to stop them I began to strike them and shouted to them to stop.' Thus far we are reminded of the earlier

[1] Romans ii, 4.

phase in Ezechiel's career; in what follows we see a re-
flexion of the later. 'Not with blows,' was Christ's admo-
nition to Don Bosco, 'but with gentleness and kindness must
you win these friends of yours. Speak to them of the
hideousness of sin and the beauty of virtue.'[1] Prophets
and apostles appear to be one in this: they begin by
resisting, and end in accepting, friendship. But if Don
Bosco was granted to see—as he certainly did see in his
inaugural vision—wild beasts being turned into lambs,
then this is where the likeness between the two servants
of God is found to fail. Ezechiel's wild beasts merely
roared less and yawned more: they can hardly be said
to have turned entirely from their evil way. Treating
the prophet with a show of greater deference, they treated
the Lord with the same indifference which they had
always shown to Him. The Lord Himself makes quite
clear to Ezechiel the effect which even the altered manner
of preaching His word is to have upon the people of
Tel-Abib.

> 'The children of thy people,' He tells His servant,
> 'they that talk by the walls and in the doors of
> houses, and speak to one another saying: Come
> and let us hear what is the word which cometh
> forth from the Lord, they come to thee as if a people
> were coming in . . . and thou art to them as a musi-
> cian's song which is sung to them with a sweet and
> agreeable voice. They hear thy words and do them
> not.'

Evidently the people understood. It is hard to see how
the critics can say that Ezechiel's message was too
involved for Tel-Abib: the exiles simply drank it in.
But that is all they did with it. In the quiet hush of
twilight they leaned against the walls of their cottages
and listened to the soothing word of forgiveness; they
gathered in doorways to discuss Ezechiel's latest sermon

[1] Jorgensen, *Don Bosco*, pp. 28-9.

they strolled by the water's edge and weighed up the pros and cons of a revealed religion; they asked each other over the melons and cucumbers of the market whether the prophet had been up to standard the night before. 'Thou art to them a musician's song': tears at the appropriate parts, intellectual appreciation, sympathy and even gratitude. But that was all: they came away saying how interesting it had all been.

The word of God had suffered the same treatment before and was to suffer it again later : The Word was to 'come unto His own', and His own would receive Him not. Fortunately the history of man was not destined to end with the rejection of Christ: 'But as many as received Him He gave them power to be made the sons of God.' And some vision of this must even have been granted to Ezechiel, for in the chapter following he forgets all about his own ministry and tells simply of the mission of Christ.

They will not listen to the appeal of God's servant? Then perhaps they will listen to the appeal of God's Son:

'For thus saith the Lord: As the shepherd visiteth his sheep in the day when he shall be in the midst of them that were scattered, so will I visit My sheep and will deliver them out of all the places where they have been scattered in the cloudy and dark day. And I will bring them out from the peoples and will gather them out from the countries, and will bring them into their own land. And I will feed them in the mountains of Israel by the rivers and in all the habitations of the land . . . there they shall rest on the green grass and be fed in the fat pastures on the mountains of Israel. I will feed My sheep and I will cause them to lie down, saith the Lord God.'

If the chapter about the bones which begin to live again is Ezechiel's masterpiece in the matter of description, then this one about the Good Shepherd is his masterpiece from the point of view of conception. For twenty verses—from verse eleven to the end—there is a sublimity which we would hardly expect to find in the writings of any Old Testament writer with the possible exception of Isaias. Surely Our Lord must have wished us to recognise whose words it was He was echoing. The Gospel of St. John finds a herald here: 'I will seek that which was lost, and that which was driven away I will bring again. And I will bind up that which was broken and I will strengthen that which was weak.'

The chapter closes with a magnificent promise from the Father:

> 'I will set up one Shepherd over them . . . even my servant David: He shall feed them and He shall be their Shepherd. And I the Lord will be their God, and My servant David the Prince in the midst of them. I the Lord have spoken it. I will make a covenant of peace with them . . . and I will make them a blessing round about My hill, and I will send down the rain in its season, and there shall be showers of blessings . . . and they shall know that I the Lord their God am with them, and that they are My people, the house of Israel . . . and you My flocks, the flocks of My pasture are men. And I am the Lord your God, saith the Lord God.'

So the Saviour of the race is to be a Prince and a Shepherd at the same time: a David with a limitless kingdom and a sanctified flock. A covenant of peace will be established and every blessing will flow down from the holy hill of Calvary. Then shall the title of the Promised Land be verified for ever—a reward will it be to its inhabitants and no longer a reproach.[1]

---

[1] The two chapters which come between what we have just been considering and the 'bones' chapter contain some exquisite passages but since they do not materially affect the story they will here be passed over without comment. If we want, however, to dwell upon the thought of God's tenderness towards His creation we could hardly do better than pick out some of the verses in chapter xxxvi and use them for purposes of

prayer. 'I will take you from among the Gentiles and will gather you together out of all the countries, and will bring you into your own land. And I will pour upon you clean water and you shall be cleansed . . . and I will give you a new heart and will put a new spirit within you; and I will take away the stony heart out of your flesh, and will give you a heart of flesh. And I will put My spirit in the midst of you, and will cause you to walk in My commandments.' (24-27) 'You shall be My people and I will be your God . . . and the nations that shall be left round about you shall know that I, the Lord, have built up what was destroyed and planted what was desolate . . . that I the Lord have spoken and done it' (28, 36). 'Moreover, in this shall the house of Israel find Me, that I will do it for them; I will multiply them as a flock of men, as a holy flock, as the flock of Jerusalem in her holy feasts . . . and they shall know that I am the Lord' (37, 38).

CHAPTER XV

THE VISION OF THE BONES

I

WE have seen how the second phase in Ezechiel's life of prophecy began with an instruction from the Lord; it was also introduced, as the first phase had been, with a vision. The passage which describes the vision is a long one but it is so full of point that we must give it all; it can however be broken up for purposes of comment.

'The hand of the Lord was upon me and brought me forth in the spirit of the Lord and set me down in the midst of a plain that was full of bones. And He led me about through them on every side. Now there were very many upon the face of the plain, and they were exceeding dry. And He said to me: Son of man, dost thou think these bones shall live? And I answered: O Lord, Thou knowest. And He said to me: Prophesy concerning these bones, and say to them: Ye dry bones, hear the word of the Lord; thus saith the Lord God to these bones: Behold I will send spirit into you and you shall live. And I will lay sinews upon you, and will cause flesh to grow over you and will cover you with skin; and I will give you spirit and you shall live, and you shall know that I am the Lord your God.'

Some would have us believe that the valley was a real one and that Ezechiel actually saw bones. Surely the whole scene was witnessed ecstatically, and not corporally and geographically. The prophet was not taking occasion of a barren valley strewn with bones to preach a homily to his people; clearly he was transported in mind to a valley of the spirit where the bones of Israel's nationality were viewed as mystically—that is to say morally and spiritually—scattered and dry. The Chosen Race, as a race, was extinct. But its relics remained, bleached and exposed, to disfigure the land; 'dry' because the devotion of the faithful was arid. Hopeless of a revival, the marrow of Juda's faith had withered . . . 'Our hope is lost, they say, and we are cut off.'[1]

The Lord asked the prophet a question: could these bones come to life again? Ezechiel's answer was the same as John's in the Apocalypse;[2] both men were guarded in their replies. For Ezechiel to have said 'Yes, Lord, they can' would have supposed a knowledge of the Books of Daniel and Job from which it would not have been easy to draw at a moment's notice.[3] On the other hand to have said 'No, Lord, they can't' would have implied the same lack of trust as that shown by the rest of Juda. 'Thou knowest, Lord,' was clearly the best thing he could have said.

> 'And I prophesied as He commanded me. And as I prophesied there was a noise, and behold a commotion; and the bones came together, each one to its joint.'

This is a tremendous vision. Somehow the idea of sound is better expressed in Ezechiel than in other sacred writers—Nahum not excepted. Between the sky-cracking claps of thunder we can hear the rattle of bones as they come together with the impact of obedience. Not an empty socket, not a finger-bone out of place. There is no mention of rain but we feel sure that a downpour followed close upon the thunder and the earthquakes; we seem to hear the water beating down upon the parched valley until eddies of it swirl and bubble round the ankles of an innumerable army of hitherto dry skeletons.

But only for a minute are they skeletons:

> 'And I saw, and behold the sinews and the flesh came upon them, and the skin was stretched out over them . . . but there was no spirit in them.'

There they stood, these bodies, simply waiting to become alive. The spirit only was wanting. Surely

---

[1] 11.   [2] vii, 14.   [3] Daniel xii and Job xiv.

H—e

there is a link here between Ezechiel and Genesis? It is as if a repetition of God's creative act were needed for the restoration of the body of the faithful . . . the material is prepared, but for the making of the new man there must be the breath of God. And is there not also a purely symbolical interpretation to the progressive bestowal of life? Often enough there is the body of religion when at the same time the soul is lacking: knowledge has seen to it that every sinew is in position and that there is skin to cover the frame, but that is as far as it has got. Love is absent. And it is the spirit of Love—God's Spirit—which gives life.

'And He said to me: Prophesy to the spirit, prophesy, O Son of man; and say to the spirit: Thus saith the Lord God: Come spirit from the four winds and blow upon these slain, and let them live again. And I prophesied as He had commanded me, and the spirit came into them and they lived . . . and He said to me: Son of man, these bones are the house of Israel; they say: Our bones are dried up and our hope is lost, and we are cut off.'

A rush of air swept down upon the lifeless bodies 'and they lived.' We can imagine a great silence following. Surely by this time the earthquake had ceased its din. Surely the rain had stopped short in the climax of its downpour, and the sun had shone down through parted clouds upon the drenched and sparkling hills and the flooded valley. We see a great host of men standing silent before the face of God. There is no sound now but the little soughing noises which are made by a thirsty earth. . . .

'*Can* bones live again?' we imagine the Lord repeating to his prophet in the stillness. 'Lord, Thou knowest' would be the whispered reply, and this time would be added—'that they can.' 'Son of man, these bones are the house of Israel' . . . the Christian Phœnix will rise from the ashes of Israel; God has not ceased to breathe.

II

The whole thing is so short: eleven verses. And what are not its possible applications? It can stand for dead souls as well as dead races; it can apply to an ideal that has been scattered and wasted as well as to a faith that has dried up in the valley of the soul. It can apply to a devotion or a friendship or a project or a prayer; it can apply to anything that has petered out under the glare of the sun. *But the bones can live again.* We may not say, as Juda said, 'we are dried up, our hope is lost.' Our hope is *not* lost, we are *not* 'cut off'—permanently.

Sometimes we look back upon our lives and a flash of white light shows us what once we were. In the valley are all those resolutions, those innocences, those fervours which were so very much alive at one time but which now are bones. . . bleached, dead, dry bones. The gospel, a dry bone. The missal, a dry bone. The catechism, a very dry bone. The rosary, a lot of little dry bones. The figure on the crucifix even—is *that* a dry bone? Is it a skeleton and not a Man? And what about ourselves? Are we too without life, dry and marrowless, fit only to be thrown all anyhow upon the heap of waste material in the loveless valley of neglected grace? If such are our thoughts, then 'hear the word of the Lord, O ye dry bones, *ye shall live* . . . I will put My spirit in you, and ye shall know that I the Lord have spoken it.'

III

Thus when we hear (as we so often do hear) the invocation which asks 'send forth Thy Spirit and they shall be created, and Thou shalt renew the face of the earth' we can recall the vision of Ezechiel. We can recall also its fulfilment: God *did* send forth His Spirit, His people *were* created anew, and the face of the earth smiled beneath the sunshine of His favour.

CHAPTER XVI

ANOTHER HISTORICAL INTERLUDE

WE closed the foregoing chapter with the prophet's vision, but in the Prophecy the text runs straight on. Ezechiel is told to get busy again with another sign.

This time the command was to take two sticks and splice them together, explaining to Tel-Abib that the two tribes of Israel would so be united in a single kingdom at the ultimate restoration. 'And,' the Lord went on to tell His servant, 'One King shall be king of them all.' This will be the New David Who is appointed Shepherd of the flock. The land where the flock is to have its pasture is again to be the land of Jacob; the fold will be established there for ever and it will be there that God's promise will reach fruition.

> 'I will multiply them and will set My sanctuary in the midst of them for ever. And My tabernacle shall be with them; and I will be their God and they shall be My people. And the nations shall know that I am the Lord, the sanctifier of Israel.'

These two verses have been quoted to show that the Jews still needed reassurances as regards their promised immunity from hostile aggression. The next two chapters in the text are a confirmation of this guarantee. Ezechiel announced that the unbelieving races of the remote north would never be able to break up the reunited kingdom in the south. The chief cause of anxiety, Gog, would himself be destroyed in the attempt to subdue the New Juda. This section of the Prophecy bristles with allusions of which some at least must be followed up.

In the first place we should note that the predictions relate to the distant future and not to any onslaught which needed to be provided against at once. The whole treatment of this particular evil is quite different from the way in which earlier on Ezechiel had handled the Baby-

lonian question. The present section refers to a time when
the Chosen People will be so far established in holiness
as to be able to meet God with a spirit undivided by
false worships and loyalties.[1] There are critics, incidentally, who rule out these three chapters as not being the
work of Ezechiel.

We should notice also that the fear of invasion was not
something new in Judea. Certainly Ezechiel's warnings
did not inspire this somewhat vague anxiety; there was
current in Palestine at this time an idea amounting almost
to a superstition which gave to the personality of this
mysterious individual Gog a power of winning to his
side all the non-Jewish peoples of the world. A combined
attack was thus anticipated. Sheba, Dedan, Tarsis, were
to be the main assistants in this all-Palestine pogrom
which was to be engineered by Gog. The Jews, then,
were afraid of attack from the south as well as from the
north, and it was this fear which gave Ezechiel cause to
insist on a greater act of faith. The Lord, repeated
Ezechiel, would prevail over Gog and his allies.

> 'And the word of the Lord came to me saying:
> Son of man, set thy face against Gog, the land of
> Magog, the chief prince of Mosoch and Thubal.
> Prophesy of him and say: Thus saith the Lord God:
> Behold I come against thee, O Gog, and I will
> turn thee about and I will put a bit in thy jaws . . .'

Here follows the best part of two chapters dealing with
the ambitious and very nearly successful schemes of this
person Gog. So nearly will Palestine come to being
dominated that the hosts of enemy cavalry will 'come
upon Israel like a cloud' but in the end Gog will find
himself 'turned about and led out.' 'I will break thy
bow in thy left hand,' is the Lord's message, through
Ezechiel, to Gog, 'and I will cause thy arrows to fall
out of thy right hand.' And so on, and so on, and so on.

[1] xxxix, 11-16.

Now who was this menacing figure, Gog? There are several views to choose from. It is possible that 'Gog' is not a proper name at all and that the word simply represents the governing spirit of the future anti-Israel coalition. The names of the countries united under Gog are so widespread that another Chaldean or Assyrian domination is ruled out from among the possibilities. And then if we take it that Gog is a person and not a group of nations, there are a number of people with whom he can be identified. He may be Gyges king of Lydia (who is called 'Gu-Gu' in the records of Assyria); this man was Assurbanipal's contemporary and therefore exercised his power round about the middle of the seventh century B.C. Again Gog may have been a somewhat nebulous monarch called Gagi who ruled a kingdom north-east of the Tigris. There is also a king Gagaia with whom Gog may possibly be identified; Gagaia ruled an undefined territory somewhere between Cappadocia and Media.[1] So much for these possible Gogs who lived before and not after the time of the prophecy. If these men ruled *before*, it might be objected, why call Ezechiel's statements regarding them a 'prophecy'? Indeed why should Ezechiel have referred to them at all? In answer it is suggested that one or other colossus of the past, some superman with whom the world was familiar, was projected by Ezechiel into the future. The evils which the prophet predicted were certainly not past evils but the name which he gave to their originator may quite well have been the name of a recent and recognised despot. At any rate whoever he was or whatever he was, his death and burial (or, alternatively, the decline and extinction of the movement) were prophesied by Ezechiel to take place at some spot on the eastern side of the Dead Sea.

[1] The Greeks have made him out to be Mithradates VI, Eupator Dionysius of Pontus; the Jews, in their later writings, simply call him the Anti-Messias—with us, the Antichrist.

As regards Magog, the name which is always bracketed with Gog, most commentators seem to be agreed that this was not a person but the place or people which should owe allegiance to Gog.[1] Both names come again in the Apocalypse of St. John.

The proximate identifications do not matter much, it is the prophecy's remote implications that are important—namely that the forces of unbelief will one day combine to make a supreme effort at throwing over the Faith, and will not be able to manage it.

When Ezechiel has finished with the taking of Gog he goes on in an almost playful way to warn Gog of the defeat he is in for. Take care, Ezechiel seems to say, God and I know exactly what you are going to do; but you had much better take advice while there is time, and give up the idea. The Israel which you will come up against is not going to be the Israel which history might lead to expect: it will be a 'secure' people . . . 'And I will hide My face no more from them, for I have poured out My spirit upon all the house of Israel, saith the Lord.'

Perhaps without justification has this chapter been called an 'historical interlude.' The truth of the matter is that the historical references contained in this section of the Prophecy cannot with any degree of certainty be commented on at all. The Gog invasion is not yet over. Perhaps it has not yet begun. At any rate an adequate commentary upon the references in Ezechiel will be possible only if on the Last Day a competent historian has managed to get all his facts together and is thoroughly conversant with the Apocalypse and the Prophecy of Ezechiel.[2] We have St. Paul's support in our belief that

[1] Cheyne, however, takes Magog to be a Babylonian deity called Migdon. St. Augustine takes the widest view of all and says that Gog and Magog mean the same thing: barbarism in general.

[2] Swete's edition of the Apocalypse gives 29 examples of similarities which exist in the two inspired Books. Redpath gives 38. In thought, in imagery, and in style St. John is found to follow Ezechiel to a very marked degree. It is interesting to note further (as Redpath points out) that

Ezechiel's words are still to find fulfilment: 'Let no man deceive you,' the Apostle tells his friends who are expecting a speedy dissolution of the world, 'for unless there come a revolt first and the man of sin be revealed, the son of perdition, who opposeth and is lifted up above all that is called God . . .'[1] Unless this Antichrist come and be destroyed, how shall the true Christ be everywhere recognised as having triumphed?

Ezechiel does not appear to have influenced any New Testament writer apart from St. John. Anyone for whom Scriptural parallels have a fascination should read Ezechiel with a marker in the Apocalypse.

[1] 2 Thessalonians ii, 3.

CHAPTER XVII

THE NEW JERUSALEM

I

WE have now reached the section of the Prophecy which is roughly covered by chapters forty to forty-eight. We have passed the last narrative portions of the Book, and from here until the end there is nothing but sheer vision; even the parable and the indictment are dispensed with. Less space can be devoted to these last nine chapters than to what has gone before, because the text, though illuminating in many ways, throws no very new light upon the prophet's life or work. Most of it is to do with the measurements of the Ideal Temple, together with all that relates to the Temple. Instead of moral teaching as hitherto the prophet lays down conditions for the form of worship to be observed at the Restoration.

The date which is given in the superscription shows that some twelve years had passed since he had last spoken to the people. From 584 until now in 572 Ezechiel seems to have devoted himself not only to a silent ministry (which, on account of his early experiences, was no new thing) but to a signless ministry as well. We would like to know what form of work for souls he undertook at this time; we can hardly think of all that zeal and energy lying idle. Perhaps Ezechiel devoted himself exclusively to the contemplative life. Certain it is that by the year 572 (the time with which we are now to deal) his spiritual state had reached a very high mystical level indeed. But if in the latter part of his Prophecy the preacher is over-shadowed by the visionary, it is the visionary who sees things through a magnifying glass. Ezechiel's pages are dense with detail.

II

The prophet's vision of the nation's restoration was, as the title of this chapter indicates, woven about the centre

of Juda's former life—the Temple. This dream, translated into the inspired words of his Prophecy, would have
excited more than the mere academic interest which
perhaps it excites in us. The blood of sacrifice may almost
be said to have flowed in the veins of Juda, and no
amount of exile had power to effect a complete trans-
fusion. We must remember that the Jews of the Chaldean
exile were, in spite of everything, a more truly Jewish
lot than any of the other groups resulting from the disper-
sion. They, better perhaps than the colonists in Egypt
or elsewhere and certainly better than we of a completely
different tradition, would have been familiar with the
Temple-idiom employed by Ezechiel in these concluding
chapters. Liturgy-starved for twenty years, the people
for whom the prophet wrote in 572 B.C. still remembered
and—what is more surprising—still wanted to hear the
language of the sanctuary.

In connexion with the above I do not think I can do
better than quote from the work of Professor Lods already
referred to. 'From the religious point of view, the exiles
in Babylon were in much worse straits than the refugees
in Egypt. It was a recognised principle among all the
Israelites, whether they followed the old popular religion
or were disciples of the prophets, that Jahweh would
only accept the worship offered up in the Holy Land.
Exile therefore necessarily entailed a suspension of
sacrifice. Popular Jahwism, as practised by most of the
Jews in Egypt, managed to avoid this result by bringing
earth from Palestine and building an altar upon it, as
Naaman had done, or else by asking the gods of the
strangers to cede a plot of ground to Jahweh, as Solomon
had done for the deities worshipped by his wives, and
the Egyptian gods for the Canaanitish gods in the days
of the rule of the Pharaohs. It was doubtless in consequence of some such arrangement that the Jewish settlers
in the Elephantine had built a temple to Jahu near the
first cataract. It may be that some of the settlers in

Babylonia had a similar plan which they submitted to the prophet Ezechiel, and that they finally erected a temple at Kasiphia, where in the time of Ezra there lived a great number of Levites and temple servants, and which is twice described as *maqom*, "place," a term which can also mean "holy place," like the Arabic *maqam*. . . . After 586, Ezechiel found himself confronted by an entirely new state of affairs. He was no longer faced with a nation which turned a deaf ear to his appeals, one which was living in a fools' paradise, whose illusions must be shattered and whose pride must be brought low; instead they turned to him like sheep without a shepherd, willing to accept his guidance, at least in theory, looking to him for consolation. His task was no longer to predict the overthrow of the State, but to foretell the future resurrection of the nation and to pave the way for it.'[1]

III

The vision of the Temple is introduced by an account of how Ezechiel was transported in spirit to his native land where, accompanied by an angel, he was shown the dimensions of the house of the Lord. In the angel's hand were a measuring reed and a line of flax; these things were also, incidentally, the insignia of the Babylonian architect. Several other details about the vision can be traced to a Babylonian influence; it is this which has given rise to the theory among the sceptics that the whole thing was a piece of pure invention on Ezechiel's part, and that he simply borrowed all his material from what he saw about him in Chaldea. Which is sheer nonsense. Ezechiel's conception of the Temple of the Restoration is an essentially Jewish conception. In fact it is an essentially Ezechiel conception. The fact that Ezechiel wrote of specifically Hebrew concepts using Babylonian characters does not detract from the Hebraic nature of the concepts. Indeed it adds to the typically Ezechiel way of going

[1] *The Prophets and the Rise of Judaism*, p. 218, 219.

about it. Just as it is characteristic of Ezechiel to be hopelessly vague and strictly accurate in the same chapter, so it is characteristic that he should be essentially Hebrew and accidentally Chaldaic in the same chapter. It does not mean that he took over a Chaldaic concept and gave it a Hebrew form, it means that he took over a Hebrew concept and gave it an Ezechiel form. Critics make the mistake of thinking that whatever is not strictly Jewish is therefore strictly Babylonian. But the terms are not mutually exclusive. The opposite of Jewish is not Babylonian, the opposite of Jewish is *not*-Jewish. When a writer uses a foreign language which has become as familiar to him as his own he is not going back on his native language, he is merely expressing himself in the way which comes easiest to him. Or as Chesterton says more pithily: 'Whether a man chooses to tell the truth in long sentences or short jokes is a problem analogous to whether to tell the truth in French or German. Whether a man preaches his gospel grotesquely or gravely is like the question of whether he preaches it in prose or in verse.' The point about Ezechiel is that he preached his gospel sincerely, and therefore did not worry in the least as to whether or not he did so with a Babylonian accent.

The Temple shown to the prophet in his vision was modelled on Solomon's but carried out on a more elaborate scale. The Temple enclosure was protected by a strip of land which separated it from the less hallowed territory of its surroundings. The inspection was so thorough that Ezechiel was able to note the minutest details. Having seen all that related to its construction he saw the 'Glory of the Lord' return to the Temple as, twenty years before, he had seen the same Glory depart. Ezechiel was then instructed upon various points of ritual to do with the sacrifices and Levitical purifications. The height of the mystical experience seems to have been reached when the prophet was shown the healing stream which flowed from the Temple's threshold.[1] From under the altar this river was seen to make its way, swelling in volume and fertilising the country through which it passed to the Dead Sea which it finally sweetened with its own purity. From then onwards fishes were able to live in the waters of the Dead Sea, and fruit trees were able to grow in the soil surrounding it. Some of its salt, however, was seen to remain on its banks.[2] When we read of this last detail we jump at an obvious mystical interpretation. 'Ah,' we say, 'there will always, then, be a deposit of its native bitterness in Israel; even the restored people, washed clean by the life-giving waters of the Temple, are not going to be altogether sweet-natured when the time comes.' Quite possibly not, but the salt in Ezechiel's vision would not justify the conclusion. The salt here means something quite different, and its mention is moreover another instance of the prophet's flair for exactitude. Salt—a certain amount of it—was required for the liturgy. Besides which, anything *entirely* sweetened (if we are still looking for mystical interpretations) would be insipid; seasoning of some sort is required for perfection.

Having had the stream pointed out to him and its miraculous effects explained, Ezechiel was next shown the new distribution of territory. There was to be an abolition of the old arbitrary lines of demarcation. The tribes of Israel were now to have each its own allotted portion, every tribe an equal area of land, the central position being occupied by the priests.

The vision came to an end where it had begun—at the mountain of Sion. From here, before the vision was

---

[1] In the twentieth chapter of the Apocalypse we have the same idea of the river of grace. It is the same stream which the Church commemorates in the *Vidi Aquam* of Paschal Time.

[2] Today abou 18,000 tons of salt are yielded annually from the region round the Dead Sea. The main salt quarries are at Jebel Usdum, some little way south of Engeddi.

lifted from him, Ezechiel was able to measure the New
Jerusalem and so to show to future generations that the
City of God stood (as it is claimed in the Apocalypse to
stand) four-square upon its bed of rock. We are in no
danger here of mistaking the symbolism: this outward
symmetry is surely to be taken as a sign of the Church's
inward order. Underlying Ezechiel's concern for archi-
tectural perfection there is always his still greater concern
for moral perfection. As a builder he is primarily a
builder of temples not made with hands. In the last
phase of all—the description of the Holy City's gates—
this is amply illustrated. There were to be twelve of
these gates, each dedicated to a tribe. Between them
they watch over the City of God. Twelve tribes, once
scattered, are now united in a single purpose; twelve
tribes, once the occasion of Israel's desertions, are now
the occasion of Israel's return.

Was there ever such an ardent Zionist as Ezechiel?
We find ourselves saying the same thing of each prophet
in turn—particularly we find ourselves saying it when
we read Isaias, Jeremias, Aggeus and Zacharias—but
was there any one among them who took so much to
heart his city's sins, trials, efforts and destinies? Dr.
Barnes concludes his excellent study on Ezechiel in the
New Commentary on Holy Scripture by saying that the prophet
saw Jerusalem 'built "as a city that is compacted together;
whither the tribes go up." [1] The name of the city, given
in the last (Hebrew) words of the book, closes one
important line of thought which marks this prophecy.
Jehovah solemnly forsook His city and summoned the
Chaldeans to destroy it. But He is to return to it with
equal solemnity, and to dwell once more in His Temple.
So the city is to be called by all who see it, *Jehovah-
shammah*, "Jehovah is there".' But though Zionist to the
core, Ezechiel is still deeper a Jahwehist. In his bitter
separation from the Holy City and its Temple he has

[1] Psalm cxxii, 3, 4.

learned a great lesson: that no separation is so bitter as
the separation of the soul from God. The altar may be
destroyed, the sanctuary may lie open to the heavens,
the priests may be scattered to the four winds, but if
the soul is still reflecting the Image of God then the
Temple still stands. 'Know you not that you are the
Temple of God and that the Holy Ghost dwelleth in
you?'[1] Ezechiel came in the end to see that God could
manifest Himself as well in Babylon as in Jerusalem,
that His *essential* Glory was not to be localised, that
men might worship Him 'not on this or that mountain
but in spirit and in truth.'[2] As a consequence of his
own isolation and of the Lord's revelations to him
Ezechiel came to feel eventually that (again to quote
from, I think, Chesterton, though I cannot find the place)
it was a far more satisfactory thing 'to have God without
the Temple than to have the Temple without God.'

[1] 1 Corinthians iii, 16.   [2] John iv, 21, 23.

CHAPTER XVIII

THE DUAL PERSONALITY EXAMINED

I

READERS who have gone through their Ezechiel from cover to cover cannot have failed to notice that the last section (the eight chapters which we have been considering in the foregoing pages) is quite different in character from what has gone before. The change is so marked that one can hardly help feeling that there must have been two writers on the work after all. In the course of this book the question of the dual authorship has been touched upon (lightly) quite often. The time has now come when the ghost of this 'second' Ezechiel must be laid.

It is claimed that such a matter-of-fact handling of such a matter-of-fact subject (bricks and mortar) bears no relation to the flights of mysticism, morality, oratory and imagery that have gone before. In other words it might be held that Ezechiel's ideal Temple is not a mystical concept but an architect's plan; we (it could be suggested) are the people who attribute the symbolism, Ezechiel—or the writer of the last eight chapters—is concerned with the ruler and set-square. We have already seen (several times) that the mystical-moralist showed an unexpected tendency to be practical; on top of this we have claimed that the practical architect showed an equally unexpected tendency to be mystical. Thus if we can prove that the Jekyll and Hyde make up the one man it follows that the Temple vision was a vision of the highest mystical order. Let us approach the matter from this end first—the vision end—and attempt to show that the whole thing is based on a mystical and not a material concept. For this it will be no good going through a list of points about the vision which admit of a spiritual interpretation; such interpretations—as, for example, of the life-giving river

and the city gates—might be regarded as arbitrary.
So, taking another line, it will be here our purpose to
show from the vision that Ezechiel was not so much
concerned with the design of God's house as with the
protection of God's people. In other words that he was
the 'watchman' which God had originally called him to be.

Now if we examine the text of these Temple passages
we find that in spite of a great stress upon measurements
and minutiæ the description is less scientifically practical
than it would appear to be at first sight. Thus we get
endless figures about the Temple's dimensions, yet when
we review the proposed site we see at once that there
can be no question of its ever being built. The lay-out
simply does not fit in with the geography of Jerusalem.
Thus Ezechiel gives us a river flowing from the altar to
the Dead Sea, yet when we look at a contour map we
see that such a river would have had to flow part of its
course uphill. In his account (to give another instance)
Ezechiel describes the twelve tribes of Israel neatly
mapped out in front of him; in actual fact the broken
country of Palestine would make this quite impossible.
What is all this leading to? Surely to the fact that
Ezechiel's vision of God's Temple was what it claimed to
be—namely a vision. Ezechiel did not see a temple or
a city, he saw a vision of God's Temple and God's City.
Ezechiel saw the ideal; it is we critics who spoil it all by
looking for the real.

So that if we get back to the Jekyll and Hyde problem
we see that if ever there was a visionary Ezechiel it was
an Ezechiel who sat down to work at an architect's
blue-print, and that if ever there was a methodical
Ezechiel it was an Ezechiel who knelt down to pray.
He was more than vaguely accurate (as his kindly critics
have claimed for him), he was accurately vague. Indeed
I would suggest that he went one further and was
accurately vaguely accurate. I mean that he was as
deliberate in his vagueness as he was in his accuracy.

He was deliberately careful about figures, but deliberately careless about facts—he did not *want* the ideal to square with the real. What he wanted was that Israel should look forward to a spiritual restoration rather than to a material one. What he wanted also was that, by showing himself careful over the details of this spiritual restoration, he would come to be regarded as, so to speak, the caretaker of God's house. Hence 'watchman.' If Ezechiel was in any sense an architect it was in the sense of being a builder up of Israel's supernatural life. Exactly regulating for the ideal Temple and its ritual, Ezechiel was laying the foundations of a new and more truly spiritual tradition. As (again) watchman it was the prophet's aim to preserve this tradition from the mundane influences which had destroyed the nation's spiritual integrity before. The profanations which, years ago, he had seen enacted in the Temple of Jerusalem must never be repeated in the Temple of the Restoration. Ezechiel, the watchman, the caretaker, the defender, the priest, must see to this. The New Jerusalem shall be 'holy' indeed.

II

'That's all very well,' it might be objected, 'but if Ezechiel deliberately got his figures wrong (from the contractor's point of view) in the last part of his Prophecy, why did he deliberately get his dates right in the first? Either the man was trying to be accurate all along and made mistakes towards the end, or he was inaccurate all along and made mistakes at the beginning. You can't have it both ways. You have claimed that Ezechiel was meant by God to rise above practical considerations relating to the future, and yet you insist that he was scrupulously careful about equally non-essential details relating to the past. There is inconsistency somewhere. But where? It cannot be in God's dealings with His servant, and it is not likely that it should be in Ezechiel's dealings with his public. The inconsistency therefore is probably with you.'

By way of answer let me do something which would be quite unpardonable in a real biographer. Let me account for my subject's inconsistency by sitting down in my subject's place. If by trying to do a work ourselves we see what other people have been up against, then by re-writing the Prophecy for him we shall find some sort of explanation of Ezechiel's conduct.

Say we are in the year 569 or so, and are considering the publication of our manuscript. We have before us on the table a mass of sermon notes, a number of old diaries, various copy-books containing accounts of spiritual experiences, and a large-scale map of Jerusalem. It is some four or five years since the first of the Temple visions was granted us, and some twenty years since we began to prophesy. The material in front of us (with the exception of the map) divides itself chronologically into three main groups: the part which comes before 586 (the date of Jerusalem's fall); the part which deals with other nations and with the ultimate peace at home; the New Jerusalem and Temple part—mostly plans. We notice a gap of about twelve years when apparently we produced no notes at all. Now it is essential to keep before the mind of our future public that the Prophecy is not the work of a single period. Have we got the dates of the original revelations? We have. Then we must put them in. If we leave them out we shall be accused of writing reminiscences instead of prophecies. The reason why we noted down the dates in the first instance was on account of the imminence of some of the events which we predicted. And in some cases the Lord Himself insisted on our taking this precaution. As regards the second group of prophecies there is of course less need to be particular; the Gog and Magog trouble was— and still is—so far off that we are in no danger of being charged with having 'prophesied' it after it was all over.

The Lord has never told us when these particular evils are to take place so we can be as vague as we like about them: we can leave out dates altogether. Now there is this last heap of manuscript—the jottings we made in connexion with what was shown us in the vision of the Ideal Temple and the New Sion. The amount of detail here is overwhelming. The question is whether to leave it all in or to take it all out. If we leave it all in, the account will be bewildering, but on the other hand if we leave it all out, the account will be misleading. Without the measurements, geographical references and so on, the vision might be taken for a revelation regarding some Temple yet to be built on Mount Sion. Whereas this is not what the revelation meant. *With* the measurements, geographical references and so on, the account will so exercise the minds of careful readers and critics that the correct conclusion will eventually be arrived at—that the Lord intends an ideal restoration as well as a material one. Thus it comes to this: if we leave in the detail the prophecy loses only from the literary point of view, whereas if we take out the detail it loses from the spiritual point of view. Therefore the obvious thing to do is to leave it in. Now let us get to work. . . .

.   .   .   .   .

I hope I have not been flogging away at a non-existent difficulty. It is thus at any rate that I see Ezechiel as he prepared his work for publication. 'No harm in copying out all that the Lord has shown me,' Ezechiel seems to be saying as he gathers the various documents into a single heap, 'and the fact that the Temple won't *fit* in the place where I've put it can at the worst only make me look ridiculous. And heaven knows I don't mind that! So long as the Lord's interests are served in the matter I am perfectly happy. When all is said and done I am only the scribe; God has inspired the work, and has therefore assumed the responsibility of its publication.' The prophet examines once again the back numbers of his many calendars. He takes down a reed from the wall and spaces out distances with it on his map. He fingers once again the many parchments on his desk. 'One has got to make absolutely sure,' he murmurs into his beard as he gets down at last to the business of revision, 'now then: "It came to pass in the thirtieth year, in the fourth month, on the fifth day of the month, when I was in the midst of the captives by the river Chobar, that the heavens were opened and I saw the visions of God. . . .' The prophet leans back. It is not his memories but his prayer that causes him thus to interrupt his work. 'I saw the visions of God. . . .' Lord, I am seeing them again. . . .

Mathematical, precise: mystical, visionary.

CHAPTER XIX

REGARDING EZECHIEL'S DEATH

I

WE have now covered the ground of Ezechiel's labours. The twenty-two years which he spent in the discharge of his prophetical labours and the forty-eight chapters which tell of those labours have been (more or less) accounted for. It but remains now to round off the prophet's life with some sort of reasonably probable description of his death. It will then be possible in a final chapter to venture a judgement upon the whole.

There is unfortunately little enough in the way of tradition which can be made into a fitting *finale* to the prophet's life. Ezechiel is believed to have been martyred on Chaldean soil. Those responsible for his death are held to be the 'princes of Israel' whom he had attacked for their idolatrous practices. It is evidently the way of exiled prophets to fall victims at the hands of their own people rather than at the hands of their natural enemies. Jeremias was stoned in Egypt by his friends, not his foes; Isaias was sawn in two by the king of Juda, not by the king of Assyria. So much for what, in Ezechiel's case, seems to be almost certain tradition. When we turn from the highly probable to the looser category of the quite possible we find that a definite site can claim for itself the prophet's death. Near Birs Nimrod (where the ancient city of Borsippa stood on the banks of the Euphrates) there is today a small Moslem town which boasts of being privileged to shelter the Hebrew prophet's remains. The mausoleum at this place, Kefil, is of uncertain date, but it was undoubtedly looked upon as an antiquity as far back as the twelfth century when it was used as a library for Hebrew manuscripts. The spot was a centre of pilgrimage at one time, and even now it is visited by Jews and Moslems alike. The foundations of this Ezechiel monument are believed to date back to the time of ex-king

Joachin's release from prison in the reign of Evil-Merodach, Nabuchodonosor's successor. The story is that Joachin's first act on regaining his freedom was to initiate a movement for the posthumous honouring of Juda's dishonoured prophet. In the tomb which was then built—Joachin came out of prison in 563—Ezechiel is supposed to have rested ever since. Thus if there is reason to believe that this legend is a true one, Ezechiel did not long survive the last of his prophecies; he finished his book just in time. Jejune though these scraps of information are, there is a certain amount to be learned from them nevertheless. We see for instance that Joachin must have used his time in prison to good purpose: he bore not the slightest malice against Ezechiel for the things which the prophet had said about him in the early days, and he publicly disclaimed any part in the crime which the princes of Israel, his old associates presumably, had committed. So the 'young lion' whose voice Ezechiel had decried came in the end to see things in a new light. Juda's dethroned monarch, chastened by the years of confinement, came to see the things of God and Juda more from the man of God's point of view than from the men of Juda's. The legend tells us also that it was not the residents at Tel-Abib who rose against the prophet; it was from Jerusalem that Ezechiel's bitterest opposition was felt in the end. Perhaps we may also infer from the tradition that the Chaldeans in whose land the outrage had been committed were far from sympathising with the offending princes; the fact that they allowed a permanent Hebrew memorial to be erected by a Hebrew nationalist king in honour of a Hebrew nationalist prophet seems to suggest that Ezechiel's handling of his delicate mission in Chaldea had found favour with the people of the land. With the above-mentioned traditions and their implications, then, we may surely be justified in reconstructing (tentatively) the conditions of the prophet's death.

II

The year is roughly 569 B.C. and the place is Ezechiel's
Chaldean dwelling-place (call it Tel-Abib rather than
Birs Nimrod). It is some months since the prophet
has seen his work through the press. He has been mildly
scolded by the leaders of the Jewish colony in Chaldea.
But only mildly. His behaviour for the last fifteen years
has been so innocent of bitterness and so retired that
gradually his fellow exiles have come to regard this
one time fire-eating zealot as one of themselves, or
rather as one better than themselves. Sincerity itself,
humble to a fault, much given to prayer, Ezechiel is
at last coming to be accepted as God's accredited agent
in the land of Juda's exile. No, the publication of
Ezechiel's Prophecy has caused little stir in the immediate neighbourhood, it is in far away Jerusalem that
the reviewers are tearing it to bits. Which is what
Ezechiel has been anticipating for some time. He has
never felt towards the faithless princes in Judea quite
as he has felt towards the fickle but far more excusable
people in Chaldea. Since the fall of Jerusalem he has
spent himself in giving comfort to individual souls, the
comfort he has tried to give to the stricken race at home
has never been properly understood. Here in exile he
has got to know his people and they have got to know
him. It makes all the difference in the world if you are
in personal contact with the people you are cursing or,
taking it the other way, if you are being cursed by someone you know. The men of Tel-Abib make allowances,
the men of Jerusalem make trouble.

One day a convoy of travellers arrives in Tel-Abib
from Jerusalem.[1] In spite of the distance they have

---

[1] We know from Jeremias as well as from Ezechiel that there was a
considerable traffic between the dispersed and the remnant. Letters were
carried backwards and forwards during Nabuchodonosor's reign, and
embassies from the Judean capital were constantly being put up at the
court of Babylon.

come, the members of this group appear to be in a hurry
to press on: they accept no invitations, they bring no
messages, they ask no questions about the political
situation in Chaldea; they are rich but they make no
purchases, they are noble but they give no names. The
inhabitants of Tel-Abib are frankly mystified. The
strangers refuse the offers of hospitality which it is only
civil to receive—let alone to offer. The caravan is not
even unloaded . . . the beasts are merely freed for an
hour or so while their masters busy themselves about
their undertaking. But what is their undertaking? Oh,
they have gone up the hill to see Ezechiel, have they?
Then there's probably no reason to be suspicious about
them: they are only doing what every one else does,
they are going to the prophet for advice. Well, evidently
he has been quick in providing a solution to their difficulties, because here they are coming down the hill. . . .

Up in the prophet's hut the flies are buzzing round
the wounds of a dying man. The princes who have
nursed their grievance over several months and across
half a continent of desert have seen to it that Ezechiel
will not recover from his punishment. As we look down
at the hunched up figure on the floor we remember the
terms of the original engagement: 'They to whom I
send thee are a children of a hard face and an obstinate
heart. . . .' We remember also that other (the Chesterton)
quotation: ' "I don't know of any profession of which
willingness is the final test." "I do," said the other—
"martyrs." '

In the stillness of the morning every sound of the
settlement below can be heard in Ezechiel's room. The
faint jingle of harness reaches us as the princes prepare
to take their leave. Through the open door which swings
on its hinge as the princes have left it in their hurry
we can see, bleached in the merciless glare of the midday
sun, the featureless country which lies beyond the mud-
hut roofs of Tel-Abib. A curtain flaps against a window-

frame; a sheet of the prophet's writing blows off the table and flutters on to the uncarpeted boards; the flies continue to buzz. There is peace in the room of the dying prophet.

> *O happy lot!*
> *Forth unobserved I went,*
> *My house being now at rest.*

Like the author of these words Ezechiel is alone when he comes to die. Among the canticles of God's prophets there is a grim similarity in signature tunes: they come to their own and their own receive them not . . . they go forth unobserved, their souls being now at rest.

Ezechiel rolls over on his back, straightens his legs, and stretches out his arms on the floor. The man of signs has given his last sign—which is the sign of the Cross of Christ.

III

A shocked Tel-Abib would have mourned the prophet's death. Perhaps Ezechiel received in death something of the love which he should have received in life. By the year 560 he seems to have been as much a hero in the memories of his people as in 590 he had been a harlequin; thirty years is not too short a time to turn an unpopular fanatic into a figure of national importance. A dead prophet is reverenced where a live one is ridiculed. We have no doubt that Ezechiel's virtues were remembered, his pieces of advice cherished and acted upon, his appearance and his mannerisms treasured, anecdotes about him retold, so that very soon he became a legendary figure, an institution, a precious memory to be handed on to the next generation as an honoured legacy. Very soon too there would have been the building of Joachin's impressive shrine to keep alive the recollection of the man whose body it enclosed. That shrine was perhaps the most glaring of the whited sepulchres which offended the all-seeing eyes of Christ.

CHAPTER XX

SUMMING UP

I

RESOLUTELY blowing away both the icy fog of scientific criticism and the rosy mist of unscientific speculation we can now confine ourselves to a few general conclusions.

That Ezechiel was a poet as well as a visionary goes without saying. We have had occasion to notice that his fantasies were sometimes so fantastic that the western mind has found difficulty in keeping up with them. If we further examine the instances of his use of imagery we shall notice that here too, as in other fields, he reveals his dual personality. There is the simple, profound, spacious poetry of the 'bones' vision and almost in the same breath the fussy multiplicity of the crocodile being drawn to land. Even when he is most truly himself Ezechiel seems to go out of his way to contradict himself. It is perhaps this rather restless quality about his work which makes him a less obviously attractive personality than, say, Isaias or Jeremias. His two brother prophets were far less orderly in their prophecies but far more consistent in their manner of prophesying. Succeeding generations have felt Ezechiel to be not very real—less truly himself than were either Isaias or Jeremias. And succeeding generations have therefore never venerated him as a person. Yet surely his very inconsistencies should make the man more rather than less real to us, more personal rather than less. Are we not usually consoled when we see a really holy man lose his temper? Do we not then feel that, though remaining a holy man, he is sufficiently inconsistent to be something like ourselves? And with regard to Ezechiel it was not even a question of his losing his temper. It was merely a question of his losing the thread.

We read the Prophecy for the first time, racing through it, and we form the impression that it was written by a

scholar, a legalist, a technician who, though normally
staid and circumspect, is liable on occasion to break out
into strange and somewhat savage behaviour. We are
satisfied that he settles down in the end to a sort of
jog-trot lonely widower existence, but we do not feel
him to have been a man to whom we would have turned
in sorrow or even in joy. He was too much the pro-
fessional priest and prophet, we think, to have been a
friend. Then perhaps we read the Prophecy a second
time, not racing through it, and we discover a new
Ezechiel. He is as changeable as before, but he is far
more human. No longer rigid, no longer distant. From
the second reading a *personality* rises up from the pages,
and we see a man who has set himself the task of painting
a series of pictures which are not to be self-portraits but
which involve a good deal of self-characterisation.
Wherever he has to bring himself into the foreground
more prominently than he would wish (as in the account
of his wife's death) he is inclined to use rigid lines and
harsh colours; where he is able to lose himself in his
subject (as in the bones picture) he is found to employ
a different technique. Besides revealing the beauty of
his doctrine, the painter here reveals the beauty of his
nature. Far from being rigid and harsh is the man who,
now by a graceful twist of the brush now by a touch of
the most exquisite colouring, is himself revealed in the
painting of his picture.

It is perhaps only when we have read the Prophecy
for the third time (or fourth or fifth) that we see the tenderness which is contained (for instance) in Ezechiel's
half-apologetic prayer for the doomed Jerusalem, in his
anxious appeal for Juda's change of heart, in the sudden
warmth of understanding which he shows when warning
the exiles of the pain they will feel when they hear of
their children's death two hundred and fifty miles away
in Jerusalem. As soon as he can he covers up these
tendernesses but he cannot altogether hide the fact that

they are there. The prophet's feelings are glimpsed at through the iron railings of his Prophecy. The relentlessness of the traditional prophet is shot through with the humanity of the traditional pastor. Taking the word of God in both hands, Ezechiel *feeds* his wayward flock. Which is what a 'pastor'—strictly—is meant to do.

II

Along the walls of the Public Library at Boston, U.S.A., runs a frieze which shows the major and minor prophets of Israel. The artist is the famous J. S. Sargent. I had often, when setting out on the study of a new prophet, sought enlightenment from a reproduction of this frieze, and had come away on each occasion with mixed feelings —mildly pleased with the picture but mildly disappointed with the portraiture. Everyone seems to agree that the paintings are good. Like all Sargent's later work (the mural decorations in question were completed at the beginning of the century) the thing is competent, sure, slick, even powerful. It is also entirely uninspired. I mention all this because two days ago I came across a passage in one of Mr. Shane Leslie's books which has changed my mind about Sargent. (Not about his brushwork but about his approach.) The book was *Studies in Sublime Failure*, and the particular failure under review was Coventry Patmore. Mr. Leslie tells of Sargent's effort to do justice to Coventry Patmore in the famous portrait of that poet. 'Realising that something still eluded him,' says Mr. Leslie, 'Sargent repainted Patmore on the walls of the Boston Library as the prophet Ezechiel. It was Ezechiel who had given to Patmore one of his greatest metaphors, that of "the bow that is in the cloud in the day of rain . . ." Between the two portraits no doubt lies the real likeness of the lonely and elusive Victorian who believed that, when he was not playing squire and journalist, he had reached the burning riddle of the Universe.' Having read this I turned again to the

Boston frieze and saw that of course Mr. Leslie was right:
Ezechiel *was* Coventry Patmore. But the point I am
really trying to make in this long digression is this: that
for Sargent to choose Patmore as a model in a picture of
Ezechiel shows that the American painter knew as much
about the Hebrew prophet as he did about the English
poet. *Patmore is Ezechiel all over again.* Mr. Leslie, with
the insight of the biographer, saw some of this. Sargent,
with the insight of the portrait-painter, saw all of it.
He saw it from the Patmore *and* the Ezechiel angle.

Patmore was—Mr. Leslie shows it clearly—a noble
idealist and an inspired poet; as such he makes a suitable
model for Ezechiel's portrait. Patmore was—Mr. Leslie
shows this too—a reactionary and a much misunderstood
man; as such again he makes a suitable model for
Ezechiel's portrait. But what, over and above all this,
Mr. Sargent saw—and saw so clearly that he could
reproduce it after an interval of years and over the space
of the Atlantic—was that because Patmore had managed
to be the squire one moment and the journalist the next,
had managed to be the family man one moment and the
lonely bachelor the next, had managed to be the meek
dreamer one moment and the fierce combatant the next,
therefore he was the best person possible to do duty for
Ezechiel on the Library wall.

To conclude what must seem highly irrelevant I would
add that for my part I seem to see a further reason why
Patmore should fittingly represent the prophet. It is a
reason which I don't think Sargent did see, but which I
fancy Mr. Leslie would. It is contained simply in the
suggestion that if the label 'Sublime Failure' attaches so
appropriately to the Victorian writer, then *as* appropriately can it be applied to the prophet of Tel-Abib.
What did Ezechiel, in his own time, bring about? Not a
great deal. And yet his failure—if you like to call it that—
was nothing if not sublime.

III

We brought in Blessed Angela of Foligno at the beginning, we bring her in again now at the end. Listening to her faithful scribe, Brother Arnold, as he read out what were intended to be word-for-word records of her discourses, the servant of God 'marvelled,' we are told, and observed with an engaging frankness 'that she no longer knew them.' Brother Arnold's accounts reminded her vaguely, she said, of her revelations, but the transcription was obscure: 'for what thou readest,' she explained, 'does not make clear what I have experienced.' It may well be that Ezechiel will have some such criticism to make about this book. So if I have got my subject wrong I can only say that I am profoundly sorry. Should Ezechiel complain, then, as Blessed Angela did, that the result is unrecognisable, I answer with the words of Brother Arnold that 'this doubtless arose through my fault because of a truth I could not, by reason of my insufficiency, take in all that was said.' I too can say (again with Brother Arnold) that 'I esteem it a great wonder on the part of God if I have written anything correctly.'[1]

[1] Brother Arnold's Second Prologue to the *Revelations*.

BIBLIOGRAPHY

Batten, L. W., *The Hebrew Prophet*, 1905.

Cambridge Summer School Lectures, 1938.

Davidson and Streane, *Ezekiel*, 1924.

Encyclopædia Britannica (various articles).

Gore, Goudge, and Guillame, *New Commentary on Holy Scripture*, 1929.

Guthrie, T., *The Gospel in Ezekiel*, 1874.

Hastings, J., *Dictionary of the Bible*, 1898.

Lods, A., *The Prophets and The Rise of Judaism*, 1937.

Moran, T., *Introduction to Scripture*, 1937.

Morton, H. V., *Through Lands of The Bible*, 1938.

Peake, A. S., *Commentary on The Bible*, 1924.

Pinches, T. G., *The Old Testament in The Light of The Historical Records of Assyria and Babylonia*, 1903.

Pope, H., *Catholic Student's "Aids" to The Bible*, Vol. II, 1930.

Redpath, H. A., *The Book of The Prophet Ezekiel*, 1907.

St. Clair, G., *Buried Cities and Bible Countries*, 1891.

Smith, Sir George A., *Historical Atlas of The Holy Land*, 1936.

Smith, Sir William, *Dictionary of The Bible*, 1896.

Story of The Bible, The, Vols. I and II, 1938.

Thomson, W. M., *The Land and The Book*, 1876.

Wardle, W. L., *Israel and Babylon*, 1925.